COLLECTED SPEECHES AND ESSAYS

1982 to 2016

ALSO BY MARILYN SEWELL

ANTHOLOGIES

Cries of the Spirit

Claiming the Spirit Within

Resurrecting Grace

Breaking Free: Women of Spirit at Midlife and Beyond

NONFICTION

Wanting Wholeness, Being Broken

Threatened with Resurrection

A Little Book on Forgiveness

A Little Book on Prayer

A Little Book of Reflections

Raw Faith: Following the Thread

FICTION

In Time's Shadow: Stories About Impermanence

FILM

Marilyn is the subject of a documentary film, *Raw Faith*, directed by Peter Wiedensmith. See the trailer at marilynsewell.com.

COLLECTED SPEECHES AND ESSAYS

1982 to 2016

MARILYN SEWELL

FULLER PRESS
PORTLAND · OREGON

Cover and interior design by Masha Shubin, Inkwater.com
Cover photo by George Crandall

Publisher: Fuller Press | www.marilynsewell.com

ISBN-13 978-0-9961040-7-4 | ISBN-10 0-9961040-7-0

Printed in the U.S.A.
All paper is acid free and meets all ANSI standards for archival quality paper.

5 7 9 10 8 6 4

TABLE OF CONTENTS

INTRODUCTION

Meadville Lombard, one of our Unitarian Universalist seminaries, has initiated a new project called Heresies—it is composed of the archival papers of notable UU women—ministers, as well as lay leaders. I was asked to contribute, so I began sifting through numerous files and boxes—materials I had carted with me from city to city to city as my life journey required.

First there were the sermons—seventeen years of them, all carefully placed in file boxes, along with the order of service the Sunday each had been preached. The sermons were in electronic form, of course, but archivist John Leeker explained to me that he wanted the paper copies, the ones with my last-minute corrections before I walked into the pulpit. There were always these hurried scratchings—I was ever trying for the perfection every writer/preacher aspires to and never completely attains. I'm unsure how many sermons I had—I'm guessing the total was around four hundred or so.

Then I turned to the other materials. "What do you want?" I asked John.

He said, "Everything."

"And that would be specifically what?" I asked.

"Everything," he said again.

"Even my diaries and journals?" I had kept these kinds of records since I was in the sixth grade.

"Yes," he said.

"Photos?"

"Everything," he said.

So the long dining room table in our home began to fill. I put the materials in stacks, to make the archival work easier: speeches, workshops, articles, essays, classes I had taught, correspondence, journals and diaries, letters to the editor, unpublished manuscripts, photographs, certificates of various kinds, etc., etc., etc.

Then as I prepared to Fed-ex the materials (eight large boxes) to Meadville Lombard, it occurred to me that some of the speeches and essays might be collected in a book. I combed through the stacks of paper again, selecting a few pieces that might be worthy of being included in a separate volume. I chose the pieces that I deemed had something of the prophetic about them—that is, some observation or claim that set them apart as calling us to a new and redemptive place, either in the culture or in our own personal lives. The first is a speech, my very first keynote address, made to the Women's Health Forum in Danville, Kentucky, in 1982. I was surprised to find how much of my thinking—especially in regard to women's issues—was already in place before I ever attended seminary, where my thinking was refined and deepened.

And so in that regard, I offer them to you—simply as pieces that might suggest to some small extent a path to a future that is hopeful, in contrast to the current darkness and moral confusion that characterize our days. That's what every writer tries to do, is it not? Just flash a bit of light to illuminate the rocky ground that we seeking creatures must traverse.

TRANSITIONS IN WOMEN'S LIVES

Keynote speech, Women's Health Forum

DANVILLE, KENTUCKY

1982

Although this early speech, my first keynote, is dated in regard to the statistics cited and the assumptions about gender, I found that it echoes many of the themes that have characterized my work ever after: references to cultural dis-ease and dysfunction, including misogyny; the use of personal stories; urging listeners to follow their call; the difficulty of valuing self, particularly for a woman; the centrality of love and work, and the relationship between the two; the continuing plea for our imagining as a conduit to new life, both for individuals and for the culture.

Thank you. I feel privileged to be here today. I want to especially thank Chris Kubale and Ida Hurt and the many other individuals who put hours and hours of work into organizing this day for us.

I'd like to begin by sharing some newspaper clippings with you. From the Lexington *Herald Leader*: "The decomposed body of Jack Een was found by police in a bed at <his> Crawford Avenue home a few days before Christmas. Een apparently had been killed sometimes in October and was not discovered until late December." How could somebody be dead for two months without being discovered? Where were his neighbors, his friends?

And from Chicago, by the Associate Press: "Some of the dozens of bystanders laughed and jeered as the man with one arm in a sling frantically tried to climb out of the way of a subway train roaring into the station, police said. But no one went to the aid of Stanley Simmons, 32, of Evanston, an unemployed cement mason and father of two children. He was crushed between the boarding platform and the third car of a four-car train . . . ." Who are these people? Are they people like you and me?

May I begin, then, by suggesting that we live in a time of great isolation and detachment, a time of spiritual sickness, of overwhelming disregard for important human questions. As a culture, the main question we ask is, "Is it possible?" and if the answer is yes, then we proceed. Other questions that we ask are, "Is it efficient" "Will it be bigger?" and "Will it be immediately profitable?" So our mountains are strip-mined, the rain is acid, the water barely drinkable, and the air at times so unbreathable that we are advised to stay indoors if we have a heart condition or asthma. And I just read in the paper day before yesterday that our pineapple ice cream is polluted. What will be next?

We live in a world that is dominated by the machine, and we think with the metaphor of the machine. Our doctors are specialists and don't talk to us or look at us: they are interested in the test results. The television set takes the place of family life, as each person sits and stares, in a passive, solitary relationship with a machine. In the Atlanta airport, a disembodied voice welcomes you and directs you on your way to the next terminal.

How did we come to live in a world like this? A glorification of the scientific method? Of rationalism? The Industrial Revolution? The loss of faith in anything except the material world—that which can be weighed and measured, and of course sold? The answer is complicated and way beyond my poor knowledge to answer. But this I see clearly: *we must begin to ask different questions.* Some of these questions might be the following: "Is it healthful for human beings?" "Is it beautiful?" "What will it mean for future generations?" These questions, I suggest, are questions which females are best equipped to ask. We know about giving life, because we quite literally carry new life within our bodies. We feed our babies from our breasts. We know about the human need for beauty, because we are the ones who have been the nest-makers, who have turned disorder to order in our homes, who have set the silver on the table to celebrate the passing of seasons, who have made the quilts and ruffled the curtains.

We need to ask our questions. We must replace the concern for production with a concern for reproduction, as Wendell Berry says in his book *The Unsettling of America*, "Production is the male principle in isolation from the female principle. Reproduction is the male and female principles in union, and is nurturing, patient, respectful of the nature of things."

Men know about production—what is fast, efficient, competitive. Women know about reproduction because our lives, our bodies are close to the sources of it. We are the nurturers, we are the peace-makers, and today we are called to wholeness in a world which desperately needs a human touch.

What is this "call to wholeness" that I speak of? What does this lofty phrase mean to this group of us gathered here in Lancaster, at the Garrard County High School on this Saturday? I'm saying that women are needed—*you* are needed. We have too long internalized the masculine view that women are weak and scatter-brained, emotionally flighty, incapable of the real business of life. It is time for us—not to behave more like men: not to "dress for success" with our fancy suits and briefcases, not to work 60 hours a week to beat out our competitor—but rather to honor the feminine principles of nurturing, emotional honesty, intimacy, co-operation, collaboration—to honor these essential human values.

"But how can I relate to all this?" you may say. "What can I do?" Each of us has an important life—each of us touches many others as we go through our days. Our choices do count. As I see it, there are two major areas in which change must take place—in our work lives and in our love lives—and I would like to explore each of those two areas in my talk today.

First of all, our work lives. We can begin by simply valuing the work we have always done, according to its real worth. How many times have you heard a woman say, "Who, me? No, I don't work. I'm just a housewife." Oftentimes the truth is that the woman who takes care of a house and small children works a 70-, 80-, or 90-hour week, whereas her husband, who is said to be "working," works 40 or 50 hours. Single women who work outside the home and also take care of a house and children essentially never stop working. Married women who work are not much better off. In dual-career families, the woman not only does her outside job, but also does an average of 80 percent of the housework, child care, food preparation, and so forth. When I hear someone refer to women as "the weaker sex," I have to smile. How many men do you know who could survive with such a schedule? And yet we take all this on without thinking we have accomplished much.

At a workshop I gave recently, one woman was talking about her coming divorce. Her husband had decided to divorce her after 16 years of marriage and was planning to marry another woman. For 16 years she had worked as a homemaker and had raised, I think it was, 3 children. And she said to me in tears, "I don't think I should ask for half of the property and half of the savings. I don't think that would be fair. I never worked. I never went out and earned the money. He did."

Personally, I am in awe of the woman who is a fine homemaker and mother. The single most challenging job I've ever had is being a mother. It is the single most important job I have, and probably the job I do least well, though I do try. This last week I was preoccupied with preparing this speech, and I forgot to do the wash. As I was cooking breakfast, my two boys (ages 9 and 10) came running in and said, "Where are the clean clothes? I don't have any underwear! I don't have any socks!" Eventually we found some underwear and socks, and they got off to school—and

I spent part of that workday feeling guilty and wondering about the relationship between children and clean underwear and giving speeches.

That night when I was putting the boys to bed and hearing their prayers, I apologized to them, and the older son gave me a big hug and said, "I'm proud of you, Mommy, for giving speeches. You're the best mommy in the whole world. You really care." Maybe he was faking it, because I know to little boys the right pair of socks is more important than any speech, but it made me feel better.

I know I have other callings, too, besides being a mother, and I'm trying—awkwardly at times—to balance out the responsibilities. For me, this call which I've been speaking of includes giving speeches, and workshops, and writing, and doing my television show. I hope my children see me as a woman trying to be whole, trying my best to heal myself and enlarge my vision about what it means to be a human being who also happens to be a woman and a mother.

Each of you has her own callings. I don't know what those are, but they involve whatever makes you feel energized and excited about living. Your callings involve whatever it is you have to give, want to give. A lot of times women are not aware of what they want to do. How many times in a counseling session have I sat with a woman and asked the simple question, "What do you want?" and how many times have I heard the same answer: "I don't know." As women, we have been trained since we were tiny tykes to smile; to please others; to exist, in fact, to serve others' needs. We have learned our lessons so well that we no longer, many of us, even know what we want, much less how to go for it.

I was interested to read about the upcoming beauty pageant for Miss Lexington and to see that one of the biggest problems that contestants have is how to smile for the whole period of time they are on stage and not have their mouths cramp. Some women go through their lives this way—on display, always cheery, always smiling—and feeling ripped apart inside. I have had women tell me about how they have been beaten up, the whole time smiling bravely as they speak, eyes filled with tears. Even when talking to me, a woman and a counselor, they were unable to show anything except a pretty face.

So the first step is to value ourselves enough to dare to ask the question, "What do *I* want?" This is *not* a selfish question. This is a question which leads to wholeness and to health. Have you noticed how a plant will turn itself and face towards the source of light? Every healthy living organism will do this—will move to get its own needs met. But human beings, human organisms, have a great capacity to learn, and as women we have learned that it's not all right to feed ourselves, to turn towards our own sources of light and life. And so women come into my office and offices all over the country and complain of depression and anxiety. According to the National Institute of Drug Abuse, 4 billion doses of tranquillizers are take in this country each year, and most of these are taken by women. Because of unacknowledged frustration and anger, women have decided to numb themselves, to not feel at all. So how do I avoid constant anger and frustration, they ask me. And I say, do what you want to do, what your body and spirit are calling you to do.

Now you may be thinking, but wouldn't I run off to California with a young lover and desert my children? No, that is merely an escape of another kind. Women who are in touch with their needs do not typically become irresponsible, but in fact more responsible—maybe not in the traditional ways other people, in particular their mothers and their husbands, expect them to—but in ways which open them ultimately to greater service, service freer of anger and guilt, service more in keeping with their gifts.

The next step after allowing ourselves to question "What do I want?" is to imagine new ways of being. How does a woman imagine herself as other than she has known women to be? As other than her mother is? As other than the images she sees daily in magazines and on television? As one of the people-pleasing women in stereotype roles?

One way is certainly just what you've done today—taken the day off to come to a woman's conference like this one—or like Women's History Week at the University of Kentucky—or like the Women Writers Conference at U.K. Here we can imagine what we could not imagine alone. There are young women and older women alike to serve as models and to encourage us by their lives. There are women here today sitting all around you who will give you energy and support just by your talking to one another and sharing whatever struggle you're in right now. Young mothers with several small children at home, trying to keep from going crazy. Middle-aged women just realizing that they're middle-aged and wondering what to do with the next half of their lives. Women going through the pain and newness of divorce. Older women worried about money, perhaps. Perhaps missing a husband who died and left them alone. There are women here experiencing the same thing you're experiencing. Get together with them. Talk. Share.

As you imagine new ways of being for yourself, surely your work is a very basic consideration. Women are working out of the home in record numbers these days. According to government statistics, only 11 percent of American households consist of a father who is the sole wage earner, a mother who is a full-time homemaker, and one or more children. So your typical family is no longer typical. The economy demands that most women go into the marketplace these days. And yet when we look at what jobs women choose, they are mostly those devalued in the market as "women's work": secretaries, clerical workers, service workers, teachers, nurses. These jobs are devalued not because they are inherently inferior—but because women do them. The wage differential is a serious one: a woman now earns about 57 cents for every one dollar a man earns. She works 8 ½ days to earn what he earns in 5. Even males and females doing exactly the same job often receive very different rewards. A female bookkeeper earns an average of $98 a week less than her male counterpart. Female elementary school teachers earn an average of $68 a week less than males.

One new way to imagine ourselves, then, if we're interested in decent wages, is to imagine ourselves in non-traditional jobs. Women are reluctant to do this, because they don't want to be thought of as "less feminine." They would rather work as a receptionist or a sales clerk at minimum wage than have a job thought to be masculine.

But let me tell you about two women I worked with in the Displaced Homemakers Program. One was a wonderful black woman named Molly, a widow, about 55 years old. She decided to become a fork-lift operator. Why? Because she could earn twice as much being a fork-life operator as she could being a nurse's aide. Ramona, a very attractive blonde in her 30's, drove a truck for a while, a 16-wheeler. She learned to drive trucks when she grew up on her family's farm, and later found herself divorced, with no means of support. So she drove a truck. Does this mean that Molly and Ramona are not feminine, not womanly, because they have these skills? I have a close woman friend who is a mechanical engineer. In Boston, I have another friend who is a pediatric surgeon. And my sister called me several months ago from her home in Mobile, Alabama, to tell me she was entering a seminary to become a minister. And why not? As Margaret Mead told us way back in 1949 in her book *Male and Female,* every society has divisions of labor between the sexes, but these assignments seem arbitrary. In some societies, boys are considered very vulnerable and in need of special care; in others, it is the girls. Some societies think of women as too weak to work out of doors, others expect women to bear heavy burdens "because their heads are stronger than men's." Sex role differences are learned, not inherent to the sexes, and therefore rigid sex roles can be unlearned—loosened or changed to suit changing cultural needs.

One exciting new role for adult women is that of student.

Typically, women who have not been in school for years are frightened of the prospect. They think that college is populated with 18- to 21-year-olds who are all clever and bright. The truth is that 25 percent of the University of Kentucky student population consists of adults—that is, people over 25. And the life experience which adults bring into the classroom usually more than makes up for the problems of adjustment. Sometimes this schooling leads to a new career, sometimes it is chiefly for enrichment.

But what is happening to the children, if all these women are going back to work and going back to school? Who will care for the children? Are these women bound to neglect their homes and their families when they take on these new roles? Again, we must imagine new ways of being, and so must our men. No longer must women be expected—and expect themselves—to do all the parenting and all the housekeeping. The men are just as much parents—and don't they live in the house, too?

A few years ago at a Gestalt conference I met a female psychologist. She was probably in her early 50's and had gone back to school for her Ph.D. after her children were in high school. During those years when she took her degree, she had dinner on the table every night, as usual. Then when she was setting up her practice, and feeling very pressured for time, it suddenly occurred to her to ask the question, "Why am I the only one who cooks around here?" She announced that she would no longer be cooking the evening meal.

That announcement shocked everyone in the family. Our *mother,* who for years has always had dinner on the table at night, will no longer be available? The family tried different plans. First they decided to go out to eat, but the food wasn't always good, and it was expensive. Then they decided to have someone come in and cook the evening meal. But it was difficult to find someone to stay for long, and so that plan was abandoned. Now the whole family cooks dinner together—the father, the mother, and the teenage kids.

This woman said her family is closer now than ever before, she is more relaxed and less resentful, and the dinner is still being made at home. A simple and workable solution. But notice who had to initiate it—the woman. The husband had become very dependent on her quietly preparing the evening meal, and took it for granted that she would always go on doing so, even when her life, her needs had changed. She had to imagine and to initiate a new way.

This female psychologist was in a conventional family structure, and made her shifts and changes within that structure. Some solutions involve imagining new kinds of family structures. Let me tell you of my experience.

Five years ago when I became separated from my husband, I continued to live with my two young sons in my Victorian house in downtown Lexington. But it was too large. I was lonely for adult company, and I was wearing myself out trying to keep up my school work, maintain that large house, and also care for my boys, including cooking them a nourishing meal every night. But I couldn't imagine having anyone else live in my house. This went on for three years.

Finally one day I ran into a friend from church who needed a place to live. I had rooms upstairs that no one was using, so I suggested that he move in. That same evening I was talking to a woman friend about this, and she said, "That sounds good to me, too. I'm tired of coming home to an empty apartment and cooking dinner for just myself. Can I move in, too?" And so she did. That was two years ago, and now I can't imagine living any other way. We share the cooking, the grocery shopping, and the cleaning. I cook only one meal a week, and yet every night during the week I have a good meal for my children and me. And my children have two other adults to interact with, which takes the pressure off me.

Of course, I choose carefully the people I live with—we have similar values. And I am lucky enough to have a large house with three bathrooms, so privacy is not a problem. Each of us has a private room, and we share the living room and kitchen. This living arrangement would never have occurred to me 5 years ago, because I wasn't ready to consider it. But my economic needs and my needs for companionship opened me to look at a new option.

It is amazing to me that 22 percent of American households consist of one person living alone (1/3 of these are women over 65). In no other country in the world are people rich enough to isolate themselves. People are social creatures—we need one another. Let us imagine new ways of living together and new forms of family.

As the family changes, so must the workplace change and be more flexible, more responsive to new family patterns as they emerge. In order for the family to be protected, there must be more part-time jobs so that neither the man nor the woman would have to choose full-time work. Maternity leave must be available, without penalty, for both men and women. Flexible work schedules, or flexi-time, should be offered whenever possible.

Of course, as Wendell Berry said one day in a class I was taking with him, "We are all carried kicking and screaming into consciousness." It is not easy to imagine or certainly to put into practice new ways. Because of the devaluation of traditional woman's work, like child care and homemaking, most men are not going to jump at the chance to take more of a part in these activities. But younger men in particular, and some not so young, are understanding the spiritual deprivation of the American male today: the job pressures which generate the ulcers and premature heart attacks; the emotional strain of having to be "strong" all the time and not to show fear or weakness or sadness; the alienation of the father from his children, so that when he begins growing older and they leave home, he says, "Where are my children? I never really got to know them. What was all that ambition all about?"

I want to speak for a few minutes about my own struggles with work. When I grew up, I wanted to be a teacher. But mainly I wanted to be a wife and a mommy. Work was something I would do to entertain myself until the right man came along. But I grew up tall and smart, two things that a girl was not supposed to be. As a teenager I tried to lower myself by walking slumped over. I tried to smile more, and not answer so many questions in class.

Even in graduate school, I was protecting myself from achievement. When I finished my Master's in English, my professor said, "Why don't you stay on for the Ph.D.? You're Ph.D. material. I'll give you an assistantship." I told him that I was overeducated already—if I ever got a doctorate, I would probably *never* get married, I said, and I refused his offer. Only in the last two or three years have I taken myself seriously as a worker.

I'm working for myself now, and all the daily choices are my own. No job has been so exhilarating and yet so difficult. I try to use my mornings for writing. Sometimes when that last breakfast dish is washed, the last crumb slowly wiped off the counter, I turn and face my work—I turn and face myself—and I am afraid. Afraid to follow my own imaginings, my own callings. I work anxiously, jumping up for more de-caf coffee, jumping up to sharpen my pencils, jumping up for a snack. There are times when I doubt that I can be strong enough, disciplined enough, smart enough. But I still feel myself called out of myself, and so I keep going, and I do find those moments of peace and of joy.

I don't know what your particular callings are, but it is important that you follow yourself in this matter. Not me, not your mother, not your older sister, or anyone else but yourself. You know—or are capable of knowing—what wholeness is for you. Trust yourself and move towards that wholeness, in faith.

We have talked about redefining work roles for women. That area, as we have already seen, is inseparable from our love lives. Here again, we need new definitions. What has been considered the ultimate form of loving—patriarchal marriage—is simply not working. Need I even quote the divorce statistics? You have heard them too many times, perhaps. In 1980 in our country there were 2,413,000 marriages; there were 1,182,000 divorces—or about half as many divorces as marriages. I understand that in California, the numbers of marriages and divorces are about equal now. Something is very, very wrong here. I believe that love as our culture has defined it is not love at all, but a cheap form of romanticism and a very dangerous lie which betrays in the end.

The betrayal, this breakdown of expectations, is seen not only in the divorce statistics, but in the violence in many marriages that are intact. In my counseling practice, I got to know a woman who was seven months pregnant whose husband jerked her naked out of the bathtub and roughed her up for being pregnant again. He had nothing to do with the pregnancy, of course. I have counseled with a woman whose husband had all her teeth pulled out because he didn't want to pay for having four cavities filled. I have talked with a woman who regularly gets beaten up before she has sex. "I ask for it," she says.

The amount of violence in our homes is overwhelming to consider. Travis Fritsch, Director of the Lexington Spouse Abuse Center, has estimated that there are a quarter of a million women and children living in violent families in Kentucky. Not in the nation, now. I'm saying in Kentucky alone. Again, something very wrong, very sick, is reflected in numbers like this.

Let's talk about how love has been defined for us. First of all, we are told that we don't deserve to be loved unless we look like the women on the fronts of magazine covers—that is, models and entertainers. We must have blemish-free skin; shiny, perfectly coiffed hair; and big breasts. We must of course be thin. It's hard when you think about it to be thin and to have big breasts, but we should try. Don't of course ever make the mistake of being old. Old is out. The truth is that we are all going to get old, unless we die first, and the truth is that a woman's character is what is important about her—her goodness and wisdom and dignity.

Second, we are told that finding the right man is an ultimate solution to the essential aloneness that we all feel as human beings. The truth is that wholeness and a sense of peace cannot come from any other person, from any man, no matter how fine he may be, but only through a woman's struggle to live well and to respect the choices she makes.

Third, we are told that our worth as human beings depends on our ability to attract and keep a man, and his worth is measured by the status of his position and the amount of money he makes. There we have a double lie. No woman is more forlorn and more lacking in self-esteem than one who has bought this lie and whose husband has just left her to marry a younger woman. The truth is that our worth as persons has nothing to do with anything outside of ourselves. We must learn to value ourselves with or without a man. Only when a woman can be content alone can she be content with another.

The problems of self-valuing for a woman are the problems of patriarchy, of course. No one sets forth these problems more clearly than does Simone de Beauvoir in her classic book *The Second Sex*, first published, amazingly, in 1949. She describes a kind of sick symbiosis in which woman is object, and man is subject. He is the measure of all that is judged, and he is the one who actualizes himself in the world. She, on the other hand, attempts to win him and please him, because living through him is the only way she sees herself existing at all. He dominates; she manipulates. He orders; she nags. He requires; she gives, but she expects in return that he take responsibility for her life. Woman and men are both exploited in this system—although the exploitation of women is the more overt and obvious. Men are just beginning to comprehend their emotional and spiritual losses.

So how can we begin to redefine love so that healing can take place? First of all, as women, we must heal ourselves. We must refuse to continue internalizing the male image of women as weak and incompetent in worldly matters. We must refuse to see ourselves as objects to be defined by our usefulness to men. We must not be afraid to be emotionally honest with men, protecting fragile egos with pretense. We must question traditional role structures which keep men and women from wholeness.

I love the way Margaret Atwood says it at the end of her novel *Surfacing*, when the protagonist, a woman, begins to move from insanity to sanity: "This above all, to refuse to be a victim. Unless I can do that, I can do nothing. I have to recant, give up the old belief that I am powerless and because of it nothing I can do will ever hurt anyone . . . . The word games, the winning and losing games are finished; at the moment there are no others but they will have to be invented . . . ."

We can begin this huge process by simply trusting ourselves, our feelings, our bodies. If your head hurts, there is a reason. If you can't walk in your spike heels, discard them. If a remark offends you, accept your judgment and speak. Take pride in your femaleness and begin to teach men about that side of themselves—teach your husbands, your sons.

Another important step is to support and strengthen one another as women. I have met with with a small group of women writers for around four or five years. I need them to do my work, and I need their emotional support when I feel my belief in myself is slipping.

Men, too, are beginning to understand that meeting in groups is important—and I don't mean to see a football game on TV. I mean to begin to talk real with one another. To dull the edge of competition. To show softness and vulnerability. Already one of my sons prides himself on not crying when he is hurt, on not showing his feelings. That worries me, because he may limit his capacity for real closeness, for intimacy, as most men in our present culture have done. I want him to be all the person, all the man, he can be.

I want to conclude today by telling you a story which was told to me by a woman in one of the groups I lead. She said that her mother called and asked her to visit an aunt who was in the hospital in Lexington. She remembered this woman as her favorite aunt, and so she went right away to the hospital, only to discover to her surprise that her aunt was in the psychiatric ward, having had a nervous breakdown. It seems that the aunt had called on a neighbor, an elderly woman, and found her alone in her house, too sick to get out of bed. The old woman was seriously dehydrated and had been lying for days in her own urine and feces. The neighbor called an ambulance and then cleaned the old woman up, washing her and putting her in a fresh gown. After the ambulance left, she sat down and started crying and apparently couldn't stop. "Is this what it means to be a woman?" she said. "To cook and clean and sew until you're too old and then you're left alone like this? Is this what it is to be a woman?"

Today I want to leave that question with you. What does it mean to be a woman?

It doesn't mean to become more like men, and set about conquering and controlling. We've had enough of that sickness. I think it means to become aware of and then to follow our own particular callings, whatever they may be. To not limit ourselves by old patterns or by new fads. To imagine beyond our present vision and make our own choices. To heal ourselves and to help others heal themselves.

Our times are marked by violence, fear, and isolation. I believe it is Proverbs where we find the words, "Without a vision, the people perish." Surely women have something to contribute to that vision. That is our call and that is our challenge.

SLEEPING WITH GHOSTS: MAXINE HONG KINGSTON'S *THE WOMAN WARRIOR*

JOURNAL OF WOMEN AND RELIGION
1992

Starting with Saint Augustine, with few exceptions, the spiritual autobiography has long been considered male territory. But in the last ten years feminist scholars have begun to call attention to female contributions to the genre. And women writers today are exploring the genre anew, for in their search for personal wholeness and social/political awareness, they have turned to narrative. Old paradigms are no longer sufficient. The new complexities of our lives and the possibilities of choice require new models, and since women have so few, we are forced to experiment, to make up our lives as we go along. It's important to hear about others' struggles, others' choices. As Carolyn Heilbrun reminds us,

> . . . lives do not serve as models; only stories do that. And it is a hard thing to make up stories to live by. We can only retell and live by the stories we have read or heard. We live our lives through texts . . . Whatever their form or medium, these stories have formed us all; they are what we must use to make new fictions, new narratives.[1]

Maxine Hong Kingston's *The Woman Warrior*

Maxine Hong Kingston's graceful and powerfully written *The Woman Warrior*[2] is perhaps the pinnacle of contemporary women's spiritual autobiography. This Chinese American writer must define herself as a woman of worth in the midst of racial and cultural prejudice in her adopted country and also in the face of the many religious and cultural "ghosts" of her Chinese heritage. The genius of Kingston's work is that although the context of her story is very specifically and dramatically Chinese American, the issues which she considers are universal: the inferior place of the girl child; the silencing of the female voice; community and parental authority that tells the female to conform; a fear of being "different" or "crazy" when internal experience doesn't square with cultural messages; a future which she is told will depend upon being "a slave" and pleasing a man, who will support her. Kingston's style not only utilizes the usual fictional techniques, but takes the reader into the realm of the mystical and archetypal. Her cultural heritage is related to her by her mother in "talk-story," and these narratives become inseparable from her own dreams and fantasies. In Kingston's *The Woman Warrior,* a very personal story, women of various social and cultural backgrounds can find the symbolical ground which unites us all.

Brave Orchid, Kingston's mother, is the dominant figure in the book, outside of Kingston herself. In fact, one might even say she tells her story through her mother's life, to a large extent. The "matriarchate" is the home in which a child grows up, dominated by the mother's relatedness, nurturing, and process. Women pattern generations through their mothers' influence. For women, the mother becomes an archetype upon which the daughter models herself and gains strength and affirmation and identity. The ongoingness of the relationship in the passing of generations symbolizes hope for the continuation of life, or immortality—and perhaps even an understanding of a feminine godhead.[3]

Kingston tells stories of other women (her mother Brave Orchid, her aunt Moon Orchid, and No-Name Woman) because her life has no meaning separate from theirs. Many other female autographs have done the same, from Margaret Cavendish and Julian of Norwich through Mary McCarthy and Maya Angelou, but perhaps Kingston does so "more boldly and more brilliantly."[4]

Kingston receives a double message from her mother. Brave Orchid had achieved her medical degree in China before the Revolution, but after moving to the United States is reduced to working in the family's Chinese laundry. She knows what personal power and achievement are—at the same time, she knows the dangers for a woman in challenging institutional and cultural power. Thus, *The Woman Warrior* begins with a morality tale about Kingston's aunt, now referred to as No-Name because she disgraced the family. She became pregnant out of wedlock, and on the night the baby was to be born, the villagers raided the family home, destroying the furnishings and slaughtering the stock. When the aunt's baby was born, she took it into her arms and jumped into a well, drowning herself and the child. "Don't let your father know that I told you," Brave Orchid warns her daughter. "He denies her. Now that you have started to menstruate, what happened to her could happen to you. Don't humiliate us. You wouldn't like to be forgotten as if you had never been born. The villagers are watchful." Kingston comments, "Those of us in the first American generations have had to figure out how the invisible world the emigrants built around our childhoods fits into solid America."[5] For the author as a child growing up, "sex was unspeakable,"[6] but the message of conformity was far more comprehensive than mere sexual conformity: it was a rule book for all of living, powered by ghosts who would not let go.

The other message Kingston receives, contradictory to the first, is that "we failed if we grew up to be but wives or slaves. Women were once so dangerous that they had to have their feet bound; 'we could be heroines, swordwomen,' seeking revenge on any who harmed our family."[7] She is told of the horrors of the

Chinese Revolution, in which many of her relatives had been tortured and killed. Night after night, Brave Orchid talk-stories until Kingston falls asleep. She cannot distinguish her dreams from her mother's stories. On Sundays the Chinese girls go to movies from noon to midnight at the Confucius Church. There they see sword women "jump over houses from a standstill."[8] The chapter called "White Tigers" is an extended talk-story about the training of a woman warrior who grows up to be a worthy avenger.

Despite all this talk of women warriors, Chinese families constantly denigrate girl children, saying such things as "feeding girls is feeding cowbirds," and "when you raise girls, you're raising children for strangers." When being punished, Kingston would cry and scream, "'I'm not a bad girl. I'm not a bad girl.' I might as well have said, 'I'm not a girl."[9] She wants to turn into a boy, but she cannot. So she determines to make straight A's and grow up to be a self-supporting scientist. There is a Chinese word for the female I, which means "slave," so Kingston refuses to cook, and when she is forced to wash dishes, always cracks one or two. "What do you want to be when you grow up, little girl?" And Kingston would answer, "A lumberjack in Oregon."[10] Since she was sure she did not want to become a slave, the contradictions between love and self-identity came early for Kingston:

> Once I get outside the house, what bird might call me; on what horse could I ride away. Marriage and childbirth strengthen the swordswoman, who is not a maid like Joan of Arc. Do the women's work; then do more work, which will become ours too. No husband of mine will say, "I could have been a drummer, but I had to think about the wife and kids. You know how it is." Nobody supports me at the expense of his own adventure. Then I get bitter: no one supports me; I am not loved enough to be supported.[11]

In *The Woman Warrior*, there is much recounting of the stories of "crazy" women who come to a no good end, either insanity or death. As a woman, one does not flaunt authority and convention without great fear of reprisal. In the chapter called "At the Western Palace," Brave Orchid insists that her sister Moon Orchid come to the United States and confront her husband, a successful doctor practicing in San Francisco, who has long since taken a new wife while continuing to give Moon Orchid financial support in Hong Kong. The doctor rebuffs the two women, and Moon Orchid finds that she cannot survive outside her known world of values. She ends her days in a hospital for the insane. Then there is the "village crazy woman" in the community where Brave Orchid was practicing medicine back in China—she is stoned to death by frightened villagers who think she is a Japanese spy, all because she wears a headdress with minors, dancing freely and flinging water at the sun. And of course, one recalls the story of No-Name. Kingston wonders if she is one of the crazy ones:

> I thought every house had to have its crazy woman or crazy girl, every village its idiot. Who would be It at our house? Probably me . . . . [My sister] was neat while I was messy, my hair tangled and dusty. My dirty hands broke things. Also I had had the mysterious illness. And there were adventurous people inside my head to whom I talked.[12]

This feeling of being an outsider is one that is universally familiar, for so often a woman's internal experience does not seem congruent with what she is told must be true. Because as human beings we are social creatures and want acceptance and closeness—and women are particularly relational—we are prone to adjust our perceptions to that of the dominant voice in the culture. Or, on the other hand, we are susceptible to self-doubt, or feelings of being "different," or at the extreme, crazy.

A related theme is that of the silencing of women. In the final chapter, called "A Song for a Barbarian Reed Pipe," Kingston says that her mother claims that she pushed her tongue up and sliced the frenum. When Kingston asks her why, she answers, "I cut it so that you would not be tongue-tied. Your tongue would be able to move in any language." But her statement is followed in the next breath with the ironic command, "Why don't you quit blabbering and get to work?"[13] Kingston goes on to say that her mother should have cut more, or, on the other hand, not cut at all, because she had a terrible time with her speech in school, where she was expected to speak English. She flunks kindergarten, and for three years covers her school paintings with black paint. In a most harrowing and violent passage, Kingston comes upon "the quiet girl," a schoolmate who is neat and clean and polite to a fault—and silent. Seizing upon the other child as an alter ego, Kingston brutally pinches her and pulls her hair, demanding that she speak. This scene goes on for pages and pages, and because of the weight and emphasis of the incident, the reader learns of Kingston's own agony of silence and repression. Afterward, Kingston takes to her bed, ill, for eighteen months.

Though Kingston's treatment of silence is contextualized in her Asian American experience, all women know something of the silence which overtakes us when we are asked to speak in the language of the oppressor, of the dominant ones, and the anger which can erupt when our experience is ignored or ridiculed.

Not only does Kingston have to learn to become a woman and not a slave, but she has to become an American woman. Brave Orchid insists upon the customs and traditions of the old country, often embarrassing her daughter and making her feel uncomfortable. At department stores, her mother forces her to bargain with the clerks, standing behind her and prodding and pinching, making her daughter translate the bargaining. The food her mother serves, such as blood pudding and squid eyes, is sickening to her. The medical remedies are strange, too, Brave Orchid keeping the pickled hand of some animal soaking in herbs that are supposed to have curative value.

The same woman, though, who is so old-fashioned in America was a powerful healer in China. The chapter called "Shaman" tells her mother's story of her medical training, including a telling episode in which the mother as a young woman faces down a ghost that was haunting the living quarters of the female students. At the end of the chapter, Kingston explains to her mother that she must leave California, and the dialogue bespeaks of love and reconciliation, in spite of the separation. Kingston begins:

> "I don't want to hear Wino Ghosts and Hobo Ghosts. I've found some places in this country that are ghost-free. And I think I belong there, where I don't catch colds or use my hospitalization insurance . . . ."
>
> [Brave Orchid] yawned, "It's better, then for you to stay away. The weather in California must not agree with you. You can come for visits." She got up and turned off the light. "Of course, you must go, Little Dog."
>
> A weight lifted from me. The quilts must be filling with air. The world is somehow lighter. She has not called me that endearment for years—a name to fool the gods. I am really a Dragon, as she is a Dragon, both of us born in dragon years. I am practically a first daughter of a first daughter.[14]

Why is *The Woman Warrior* satisfying on so many levels, when so many other attempts at spiritual autobiography leave the reader still hungry? Kingston does not demur, but rather has the courage to take on the tearing conflicts of her girlhood as an Asian American trying to find a life that is authentic and not demeaning. She avoids the pitfalls of the literal by using the ghosts as metaphors of her experience. She uses fictional techniques to render narrative passages with power and emotional resonance, never letting "the facts" interfere with the universal truth that pulls her deeper.

Perhaps in writing *The Woman Warrior,* Kingston herself is doing as her mother did, sleeping in the bedroom with the ghosts of her past, confronting that which she fears the most. This is very likely the motive behind much contemporary female autobiography: to know surely where one has been, in order to chart the journey ahead, taking what comfort and direction we can and leaving behind what we must.

Conclusion

We can expect women to continue to tell their stories in many different forms, including that of the spiritual autobiography, for we are in a cultural transition in which the traditional narrative is proving inadequate to sustain us and to guide us:

> Woman is the Sleeping Beauty, Cinderella, Snow White, she who receives and submits. In song and story the young man is seen departing adventurously in search of a woman; he slays the dragon, he battles giants; she is locked in a tower, a palace, a garden, a cave, she is chained to a rock, a captive sound asleep; she waits.[15]

If she cannot live through and for a male, today's woman must live into her own inner story and let it join with other women's to create a new paradigm of what it means to be a whole human being. Men are beginning their struggle now—largely in response to the changes in women—to determine what a mature man would look like, one who is comfortable with his own masculinity in such a way that he is not impelled to denigrate women in order to quiet his own fear.

But aside and apart from what men decide they must do, we women have our own reasons for telling our stories: (1) untwisting the strands of our lives helps us to gain a sense of identity and therefore of personal power; (2) once it reveals where we have been, the narrative suggests a path for the future, both for the writer and for her readers; (3) the themes which emerge from our life stories suggest contemporary women's spiritual autobiography, at least in this stage of cultural evolution, is essentially a search for self, a search that defines our reasons for being and allows us, then, to ground ourselves in purposes larger than our own. Relationality will always be crucial for women, and yet whether it is a relationship to a man, to children, to other women, to our chosen work, or to our God, it must be a relationship that honors our integrity of person.

For want of a story, many have perished—there are many ways of dying—because they could see no reason to go on, nor any path that seemed to offer the life-giving spirit. Or they may have violated others, in response to their own violation. We owe it to ourselves and to those who have ears to hear, to leave our silences behind and to speak as clearly and as powerfully as we can.

Endnotes

1. Carolyn Heilbrun, *Writing a Woman's Life.* (New York: Ballantine Book, 1988).

2. Maxine Hong Kingston, *The Woman Warrior: Memoirs of a Girlhood Among Ghosts.* (New York: Vintage Books, 1989).

3. Stephanie Demetrakopoulos, "The Metaphysics of Matrilinearism in Women's Autobiography: Studies of Mead's *Blackwinter Winter,* Hellman's Pentimento, Angelou's *I Know Why the Caged Bird Sings,* and Kingston's *The Woman Warior,*" *Women's Autobiography,* ed. Jelineks 180-205, passim.

4. Strange 22.

5. Kingston 5.

6. Kingston 15.

7. Kingston 19.

8. Kingston 19.

9. Kingston 46.

10. Kingston 47.

11. Kingston 48.

12. Kingston 189.

13. Kingston 164.

14. Kingston 108-09.

15. Simone de Beauvoir, *The Second Sex*, trans. and ed. by H. M. Parshly (New York: Bantam Books, reprinted 1970), 271-2. Cited in Hirsch, "Spiritual Building: The Beautiful Soul as Paradigm," 23.

THE PLACE AND FUNCTION OF RELIGION IN HUMAN LIFE

OREGON HUMANITIES
1994

Paleoanthropologists now believe that an extraordinary evolutionary step took place some five million years ago, the step that separated hominids from apes. Fossils from Lucy and more recently Son of Lucy, about three million years old, show a creature that looks much like an ape and has the small brain of an ape, but has the upright posture of a human being. At some point—we're not sure when—this creature stood upright and walked. It became able to ask the question, "Why?"

Why was I born, and why do I have to die? That's the fundamental question. But there are others. Why must I suffer so much, be subject to illness and accident and natural disaster during my time on this earth? Why do some people wish to hurt me? Why do I do violence to others? Why must those I love be taken from me?

Unable to answer these agonizing questions, people began creating ritual—making music and praying and sacrificing—trying to be reconciled with nature and with the Mystery. At that point in our evolutionary history, when we needed to make some sense of death and suffering and evil, religion was born. This is not to say that we have been entirely successful in answering these troublesome human questions, but they have remained the central concerns of our various religious traditions.

Back to the fundamental dilemma: we human creatures know that we are alive and that one day we will be dead. We can hardly imagine our own non-being, and much of the time we simply deny to ourselves that we, like everyone else, will die. But as others whom we know and love begin to die, a felt knowledge of our own mortality begins to assert itself. If we are at all reflective, the hard questions, rather easily overlooked in our youth, begin to crowd into our consciousness. We may find ourselves anxious without any tangible reason. We may begin fitness programs in order to prolong youth and health. We may seek out a spiritual path to counter the meaninglessness we are experiencing with such new intensity.

Although we may become more serious about our spiritual lives as we fall into middle-age, people of all ages have psychological needs that can be met through religion. We all are aware that we want to be better than we are, that our words and actions do not match our understanding of what it is to be a good and virtuous man or woman, boy or girl. We need forgiveness, absolution. We need a way to start over. Religion provides that vehicle.

We all have times of despair, when hope seems to flag and renewal lacks all possibility. Religion places the individual worshipper in a context much larger than that person's own pain: one is brought to see that the playing field of life is much vaster than one's own backyard. Within the mystic traditions of various religious faiths, for example, the individual may at times feel at one with all that is, and thus be released from the ego, the solitary struggle of the self. Hope, then, is not grounded in release from human pain, but in the understanding that no one is really separate from anyone else and that all pain and all joy belong to all who live.

In addition, there is the need in all human beings to acknowledge significant transitions: birth, coming of age, marriage, death.

For instance, consider marriage. Marriage is the public acknowledgment of the love which two people have already confessed, each to the other. It is more than that, however: the ceremony also brings the couple into the human tradition of the community and of the larger world. It sanctifies their relationship and their bonds with each other and binds them in a new way with all whom they now know and will *ever* know. The tears that are shed at a wedding ceremony come from sources much deeper than joy for the couple marrying. They are tears of regret for vows broken; they are tears of thankfulness for spouses living or dead; they are tears of hope and promise that lasting love is a reality of human life and not just a foolish longing.

In our particular culture, we have so secularized life that ritual is being practiced less and less. If there is no meaning larger than fact, no mystery more compelling than mere information, why bother to have a memorial service when someone dies? It is to meaning and mystery that ritual is addressed, and we need more of it, not less. We need rituals to mark loss, so that we may grieve. We need rituals to mark our joy, so that we may celebrate. These rituals make a path for our deepest feelings and join us with the larger human family.

Recently a young couple in my church lost a baby through a miscarriage at five months. The tiny baby lived an hour and a half, and was alternately held by the mother and the father until he died. The parents talked about their loss, and they wept. The following weekend, they took the baby's ashes to the coast to scatter them in the ocean and to read some words they had chosen for this special time. They marked the sacredness of the birth and the death by their words and actions, thus honoring the life of their baby and enabling them to move on more easily with their own lives. Those present in the congregation the following Sunday heard the minister recount the brief story of the couple's loss. Those of us who have living children gave thanks in our hearts for those children. A pregnant woman prayed for the baby in her womb. All of us who have ever lost anyone dear to us mourned with the young couple. We knew once again that we are a community.

Ritual can address levels of primitive, subconscious need. In India, there is a celebration in which milk, honey, and curds are used to wash images, and then the mixture is poured on the people. There are times when each one of us wants nothing more than to be at mother's breast, safe and satisfied. Such a ritual meets a psychic need of which we are hardly conscious. In the Christian religion, the symbol of the crucifix and the playing out of Christ's passion work at this same deep level as the faithful experience the blood sacrifice of the scapegoat, the death of the innocent for the sins of the many.

There is value for our psychological selves in religion, and there is value for our corporate lives, as well. Every culture evolves certain moral and ethical codes that bring cohesiveness and order to groups of people living together. Those codes need to be taught to the young and reinforced for all the people, young and old alike. It is in our religious lives that we create a model for living, that we rehearse the story we will live when we leave the church or synagogue or other places of worship and go out into the world. We often fail in living out of the model we have set for ourselves, but there is always the model to go back to, to remind us of the good, to restore our sense of right action and thought. At best, religion will set us straight, will give us confidence that we can be transformed and teach us that even our wounds can be used for the good.

Every culture needs a story to live by, a sustaining narrative that can carry the weight of our human fears and longings. Philosophy is not a large enough container for this function, for it depends on logic and ideology and can shift too easily in the winds of political and economic change. Religion has, needless to say, been corrupted by those wanting to harness its power for their own questionable ends. However, the story—the core narrative—just keeps reasserting itself like the phoenix rising from the ashes. The story varies from culture to culture, and yet there are remarkable similarities. The story says we are more than flesh.

The story says we are enfolded in Infinite Mystery. The story says love is stronger even than death. It is a story to live by. It is a story the community can gather round. And it is a story we can wrap around our scared hearts on a cold winter night.

WORKING CLASS IN UNITARIAN UNIVERSALISM

UU WORLD
1998

It was an elegant dinner party for Unitarian Universalists in a faraway city where I was visiting. Elegant but not posh, you understand. Understated. Nothing that would strain our credibility as justice-seeking people. The man seated to my left was fluent. Charming. Sophisticated. We chatted amiably about this and that. I noticed his suit. Italian silk, perhaps? Very nice. We were developing a kind of rapport. Then, for want of a better thing to say, he turned to me with a smile and asked, "And what does your father do?" I thought it a most peculiar question. I answered, "He's dead now. He was a roughneck in the oil field." His eyes opened wide in surprise. "Oh," he said. And that was the end of the conversation.

For him, the question was not peculiar. It was firmly grounded in assumptions he had made. Since I was educated and well-spoken, I must have come from a privileged background. Privilege leads to privilege. Mostly, that's so. We were in the same club, he thought. When he found that we were not, he was embarrassed. He had, he thought, committed a faux pas in asking about my father. How awkward to have a father who worked in the oil field! A father who doubtless was ignorant and uneducated. Clearly, my father did not fit at this dinner party.

My fork suspended in air, I turned away from my dinner companion—you *have not a clue*, you *with your soft hands and fancy clothes*—and for a moment my thoughts drifted back to my father. I thought of the man who had put me and my younger brother and sister through college by climbing 140 feet up in an oil derrick in the driving rain and sleet; who came home exhausted, his hands and face and clothing black with oil; who never once in his life had a paid vacation. He was a working man with a beautiful, strong body, and I was proud of him. Always was. Still am.

As Unitarian Universalists, we have now broken a number of taboos: race, sex, gender. We're working on money. But class? It's a closed subject.

Part of our discomfort comes from unfamiliarity with class differences. Most of us are middle class and upper middle class, and the way we dress and behave is not the same as that of the working class.

A man who attended our church for a while brought this home to me. He was from a Pentecostal background, and there in our formal Georgian sanctuary he would raise his hands in praise each Sunday as we sang "Spirit of Life." When I saw his hands go up, my hands wanted to go up, too! I didn't raise them, of course. I told myself that my congregants wouldn't know what to think. The truth is that I'm not any freer with my flesh than they are. I have learned not to move my body in church, so as not to disturb the Holy with my humanness. And in my careful restraint I support what is perhaps the most dangerous theological split in the Western world—that between the spirit and the flesh. It is this split that allows our culture to denigrate women, who are after all of the flesh and of the earth. It allows some white Unitarian Universalists to say of people of color, "They wouldn't be comfortable here. They're too emotional."

The man who raised his hands in praise came to our church *for a while*. Then he was gone. Just as Unitarian Universalists need people of all races and ethnic groups and theological persuasions to enlarge our frame of reference as we seek to grow in truth and to make justice, we need people of all social classes, including the working class. But the barriers are there.

We are mostly well-off, mostly comfortable. Our household income is the highest of any denomination except Reform Judaism. Hardly any of us work with our hands—we tend to be white-collar workers and professionals. And we own stock, at least in our retirement plans. Most of us have no idea what it is like to eke out a living on minimum wage. and we really don't want to think about it. We think the system works, because it works for us. But did you ever hear the single mother handing out burgers at McDonald's exclaim about how the market is doing? Who really has a place at the table?

Not only do UUs need to know working-class people and make them welcome in our churches, we also need a conceptual container roomy enough to hold our society's complex, systemic structures of oppression. I would suggest that container is class. Our single-issue approaches do not bring lasting change and at the same time may even divide us from one another.

Let's take, for example, how we have dealt with racism in our association. We have considered it a thing apart, and we have generally struggled with it where it has affected us—as middle-class people. But so many people of color are among the poor and the working classes. Can we really talk with much power or authenticity about racism without talking about the economy? About how big money owns the electoral system? About corporate media control? About environmental racism?

The fact is that we are all truly living in sin—in systemic sin. We may not have caused it, but we are a part of it. We are living in a system that provides untold wealth for a few, squeezes the middle, and leaves the bottom 15 or 20 percent in despair of any future at all. We middle-class folks imagine that the system works for us and take comfort in that belief. But we have to understand that the 0.5 percent of the population who own the wealth of the country virtually control our political life and are rapidly relieving us of any shreds of democracy.

I keep wishing the Pentecostal fellow would return. Perhaps he could help us learn to loosen up, to raise our hands in praise, to see our work lives from a different perspective. Maybe then we could begin talking about class. The squeezed middle has much more in common with working people and the poor than with the very wealthy few. It's not just "them," you know—it's anybody who has been restructured, downsized, laid off, put out, put down. It's all of us, and we'd better stick together.

IMAGINING A NEW WORLD

Service of the Living Tradition

UNITARIAN UNIVERSALIST GENERAL ASSEMBLY
NASHVILLE, TENNESSEE
2000

We are gathered here today at what is known as the Service of the Living Tradition. It is an auspicious time, for it is a time when our larger community comes together to affirm our strength and our purpose, our values and our ideals. We look back with thanksgiving for ministers who have gone before, and we look ahead to those who will bring new life and vigor into our movement.

Note that we do not call this service merely the "service of tradition," nor do we refer to it as just "the traditional service." No, it is the Service of the Living Tradition. It's the word "living" that makes all the difference. Living implies response. All living organisms respond to their environment, to their context, and so it is with a *living* institution we are called as a religious people, as we have been called all through our history, to *respond*—to be responsible to the contemporary moment. The question that I want to pose today is, what are we, as Unitarian Universalists just now in this particular day and time, at the beginning of a new century, called to be and to do? We have just heard the beautiful voices of these children—what kind of world are we going to be handing over to them when we are gone?

I know this: something new is coming. Something new is stirring in the collective psyche. It starts with the beginning of an intuition, a new consciousness pushing from within, waiting to be born. It has to do with our spiritual being. And it has to do with justice.

For me it began with a kind of restlessness and uneasiness. I have been increasingly agitated by what I see happening in this country—the social and economic indicators that I follow in the newspaper—and in fact the very real flesh and blood examples that I see all around me every day as I minister in an urban church. I had to ask myself, why are so many of our mentally ill wandering the streets? Why did the Oregon food bank have a 17 percent rise in requests last year? Why are so many teenagers cast away, sleeping in the very doorways of our church? Why, in a time of plenty? Seeing all this, I was led to examine the larger structures of oppression which bring so much suffering to so many lives. And the more I have learned, the greater my outrage has grown. As one of our congregants wrote to me, "The spiritual part of my being calls for a personal response."

I have come to believe that economic inequity—in theological terms, *greed*, which has become steadily worse over the past few decades—is the root problem which must be addressed. The abuse of economic power manifests itself not only in the lives of the poor, but in the lives of the middle-class as well. How many of us are working longer hours than ever before? Which one of us does not know of individuals who have been "downsized" after years of faithful service? How many families must have two or more breadwinners, just to survive?

But as I said, change is in the air. Alternative voices are being heard now. Voices like social critic Howard Zinn*, whose lecture so packed a hall at Portland State University that hundreds had to be turned away. His book, *A People's History of the United States*,

* I highly recommend Zinn's *A People's History of the United States: 1492-Present*, HarperCollins, 1995.

shook me and changed me. Voices like Michael Moore, the union advocate and documentary film maker who gave us "Roger and Me," again speaking to an overflow audience that caused his talk to be postponed 45 minutes until room could be found. I'm sure you read about the World Trade Organization protest in Seattle, which drew an estimated forty to fifty thousand people. All these people to protest unfair trade agreements? All these people that informed about complex issues and that angry? Environmentalists, trade union workers, human rights activists, people of many different ethnic groups—all standing together, as we have never before stood. For the more than one hundred people that our church set to Seattle, it was a life-changing event. We knew that we had made a difference. And we came away convinced that major social changes are underway.

People are waking up. What is the part that Unitarian Universalists will have in this new awakening? We can learn, and we can reach out to others in creative coalitions—one might say, *entrepreneurial* coalitions. We can work with the Catholics on the death penalty. With the trade unions for a living wage. With people of color to effect racial justice. What do all these issues have in common? Class struggle. We need to stand together, not on our own. Not my *issue* but our *issues*, for they are at one with the other. We can be the bridge that is so sorely needed. Unitarian Universalists have always had power far beyond what our numbers would suggest—so many of us have the substance and skills to lead. A new day is at hand. Where will we be in shaping that future?

I want to examine in more detail what I see happening to Americans in this time of vaunted economic prosperity. Have you ever wondered why there is so much anxiety in the workplace? In these days of mergers and acquisitions, no one is really safe.

Let me tell you Ruth's story. I'm taking this account, incidentally, from Texan Jim Hightower's book *There's Nothing in the Middle of the Road but Yellow Stripes and Dead Armadillos*. Ruth Shaver is from small-town Texas, a community known as Mesquite. She worked for Safeway for 22 years until the company was sold to Kohlberg Kravis Roberts, a Wall Street firm that specializes in raiding corporations. To lighten their debt load, they began getting rid of some big chunks of Safeway, including the 141 stores and 8,814 Safeway workers. Just like that. Entire Dallas division, out the door.

Now no one was a more cheerful and dedicated worker than Ruth. Not only did she check groceries, she trained others and helped remodel stores. She had such pride in her work that many customers asked for her by name. Over time, she had worked her way up to earn $12.06 an hour, or about $24,000 a year. Then she was dumped, with no golden parachute. Because of her union's contract, she got a small severance payment, but it lasted only a few weeks. The market for grocery clerks was glutted, and the new job she found paid only $5.70 an hour. The other 8,813 Safeway employees had trouble finding good jobs, too, and when they did find work, almost everyone had to take pay cuts 30-60%. Four committed suicide. The divorce rate among these families has been unusually high.

But Kohlberg, Kravis and Roberts are doing OK. They each had personal incomes of more than $40,000,000 the year they dumped Ruth and her co-workers. Henry Kravis became one of the 400 richest people in America. In fact, he has now become a philanthropist—and not a modest one. He donated $10,000,000 to New York's Metropolitan Museum of Art. In gratitude, the museum named a wing of its building after him.

Hightower ends this account by saying: "So Henry Kravis got the glory as well as the gold. But, you know, there are bricks in that wing of the Metropolitan Museum of Art that belong to 8,814 Safeway employees, including Ruth Shaver, who still lives in a trailer house in Mesquite, Texas."

You know, as Unitarian Universalists, we don't often meet the Ruth Shavers of this world; most of our friends don't live in trailer parks. But we can't do justice work in a vacuum. We need to learn from people who live on the edge: people who are poor, people who are transgender, children who are homeless, migrant workers—people who makes us feel shaken and uneasy because their lives are not like our own. We will learn what we must do only when we risk not knowing at all what to do, when we listen to voices we have not yet heard. We have to "leave home," in a sense, leave our comfortable ways of being, to find ourselves and our calling. We need to develop a passionate discontent, an anger that picks us up and shakes us by the neck and will not let us go. The Holy Spirit, you know, is not on the side of order and stability.

I had a recent experience that taught me some things. Because it's easy for me to intellectualize "poverty," I asked our Social Justice Director at the church, Kate Lore, who has worked with homeless people for years, to help some of us understand what it's like to be homeless. So she arranged what she called an "immersion experience," which twenty congregants signed up for. We were to sleep in a shelter in sleeping bags and then the next day replicate as much as possible the homeless experience. Well, people kept calling Kate and dropping out, the closer we got to the deadline. More than half the people dropped out, others took their places, then they, too, started dropping out. Those of you who work with people who are homeless probably remember how apprehensive you felt the first time you got involved. I, for sure, wanted to drop out. I was telling myself, "What was I thinking? I've got important stuff to do! I've got to write the sermon for the Service of the Living Tradition. Besides which, my back is not going to do so well sleeping on the floor." We ended up with 16 church members, and I of course did go. After all, I'm the minister. I couldn't weasel out.

We had an orientation that Friday evening, and then prepared for the night. I hated sleeping in my clothes, crammed in with all these other people, most of whom I didn't really know—I had no privacy. And my back didn't do well on the floor. We were up early for a simple breakfast and I do mean simple: I had a bagel and a little juice. Each of us was given a $1.00 for lunch. We gathered to select sites for visiting, and I chose the Salvation Army. I said to the group of us who were going there, "Well, that's about two miles away and over a bridge. I guess we'll have to drive." Other people kind of smiled, and then someone said, "Uh, Marilyn—uh, excuse me, but people who are homeless don't have cars." That was only the first mistake made by their fearless leader.

At the Salvation Army we prepared lunch for the temporary residents. They came through the lunch line, and then each sat at a separate table and began eating in silence.

I pick up my tray, and I look around. Just like them, I guess, I don't want to risk rejection. I see a guy who said "hi" to me earlier, so I take a chance: "Do you mind if I sit here?" I ask. He pauses and then says, "Go ahead." For a while I say nothing, and both of us have our faces in our food. Finally I say, "So how's it going?" He looks up, and for the first time I really see him. He is a man of about 50, a Native American, I would guess, with neatly combed hair that is graying, and a clipped mustache. His features are coarse, and his nose has been broken at some time in the past.

We talk awkwardly, we chat. He wants to know who I am and why I'm there at the shelter. I tell him, and he seems to warm up to me a bit. I see the tattoo of a pair of boxing gloves on his forearm. "Are you a boxer?" I ask.

"Used to be," he says. I can see from his strong build, a boxer. "I used to be the State Champion—started with welterweight, when I was just a kid."

"Wow," I say. "Wow."

"I got in trouble, though, because of my drinking. Got in trouble, and got in jail. I would get out, get drunk, and get in trouble again. I been in jail most of my adult life. I'm on parole now. Going to A.A. Trying to stay clean and sober." His eyes look hopeful, determined.

"What's your name?" I ask. "My name is Willie," he answers,

and he puts his hand forward, a hand surprisingly soft for a man of the street.

"My name is Marilyn," I say.

"Will you come back?" he asks.

"Maybe," I say. "Maybe."

All of sudden, it's not just numbers, not just statistics about "the homeless"—it's Willie. I'll always remember him. I see his face, feel his hand, hear his voice saying, "Will you come back?" And I know that, yes, in some form, in some way, I'll be coming back.

You have all seen the statistics on division of wealth in this country, and so I'm not going to spend a lot of time on that, but let me give you one figure that just flabbergasted me. It's just over the top. In the 80's and 90's practically all the wealth we generated as a people went into the pockets of the wealthiest among us. The income of the top 1 percent went up 61.6 percent. The bottom 80 percent of the population—and this includes almost all of us—gained 1.2 percent. But let's leave the numbers; let's translate this into shopping. These numbers reveal why one woman—who likely does not work at all—can go into Saks Fifth Avenue and pay $350 for a little black leather purse (on sale), while across town a minimum-wage mom has to go to bed hungry so that her children can eat.

She's one of the lucky ones. We are forming a vast underclass who are either wandering the streets or in jail. They have no stake at all in the society, and don't see a way out.

Fact: One out of 5 of our workers makes less than $6.00 an hour. That's barely $10,000 a year.

Fact: The U.S. has a higher proportion of its citizens jailed than any other country in history.

Fact: Over 20 million Americans cannot read the poison warnings on a can under the sink or a letter from a teacher or the first page of the paper.

Fact: The fastest growing population among the homeless is families. The average age of a person who is homeless? You guess. Eight years old.

As I began learning about these issues, I realized that I needed to know more about economics, and I began reading. What a wasteland! As John Kenneth Galbraith said, "If all the economists in the world were laid end to end, that would be a good thing." The basic problem with economics today is that it's trying to be hard science, and it's not. Very human problems have been reduced to sets of elaborate mathematical formulas that have no philosophical or moral container—unless one could say the assumption is that people are totally self-interested and materialistic, and only the fittest should survive. Our economic policies are based on this kind of thinking. As Unitarian Universalists, do we not believe that all people have worth, and that society should be judged not just by how much freedom it gives to the strong, but rather by how much care it gives to the most vulnerable?

This is not the first time in the history of the republic that we have been up against big money and the abuse of power. Remember the Gilded Age, at the turn of the last century? This was a time of gross economic inequity—the time of the terrible injustices of child labor, unregulated corporations, appalling conditions in our prisons and mental hospitals, and the legal bondage of women. It was a time that begged for reform, and some of the great 19th century reformers were from our religious faith, people such as Clara Barton, Susan B. Anthony, and our friend and ally Jane Addams of Hull House—which incidentally was bankrolled by a Unitarian. It was a new day. People stepped out to lead, and others followed.

We are now in a second Gilded Age. I believe that the clear and compelling issue in contemporary life is the rise of big money and with that rise, the demise of democracy. "We have two governments," writes Lewis Lapham—the provisional government, which speaks to the people through pageants, parades, and the press. And then the permanent government, which is a secular oligarchy of the rich and powerful. This government goes about its work quietly. Free expression among the citizens is fine, so long as nothing interferes with the rule of money.* Whoever gets left behind, gets left behind.

So what are we to do? We must begin to speak to one another and to listen, and then to imagine a different way. It's not just those *others* who are in trouble—it's all of us—we are all one body. We must gather in groups and tell one another about our fears for our own safety, about our loneliness and isolation, about the clutter in our lives, about the children we don't understand, about the job that sucks the life out of us, about the days going by in a blur with nothing to show for them. If we allow our hearts to speak, we will discover very quickly that we are not alone. And with that knowledge comes the sense of community and caring that will support us on our journey to a better place.

But it is not enough to speak of our pain. We must understand that our world is not irrevocably the way it is; our current economic structures, despite what some people believe, have not been divinely ordained. Human beings, just *people* have made choices, and we can make different choices. Let yourself imagine. Let yourself dream. If you could change your society, what would it look like? Who all would be included? Who would be in charge? What would your vision be?

I speak of imagination as being essential. I say this because the power of the human mind is both enormous and beautiful to behold. I believe that we can create a better way. And I speak of the imagination of common folks like you and me, because I no longer believe that the solution to our social problems will come from the top down. I do not believe that our politicians will lead us to this new world, mainly because our system of campaign

* Lewis Lapham, *Harper's Magazine*, August 1996.

financing forces them to feed at the trough of the rich. We must lead, and they will follow.

So solutions are not likely to come from Washington. Nor will they come through a particular political ideology. It's pretty clear that capitalism has won out over the planned economies of socialism, but the excesses of capitalism have led us to poverty—material poverty for many, and spiritual poverty throughout the land. We need a vision. The scripture doesn't say, "Without a program, the people perish"; it doesn't say, "Without a political agenda, the people perish"—it says, "Without a vision, the people perish."

You see, it is our vision, our changing consciousness, that will determine the shape of our world, will determine even what we are able to see. You know, every culture has a story, a kind of controlling narrative. Some wag has suggested that our cultural narrative is "BE BORN, CONSUME, OBEY AND DIE." What a scenario! And we wonder why our children are confused and restless. This is not a worthy narrative, a worthy story, to pass on to them.

But there is hope. I will share with you some of the shifts I'm hoping for, and that I see signs of already. A shift

- From economic expansion to balance
- From the plundering of the earth to reverence for the earth
- From individuality to community
- From knowledge to wisdom
- From greed to moderation
- From charity to justice

It is our passion for justice that will rekindle the social imagination. But be wary.

And I say this in particular to Unitarian Universalists, who so easily fall into the sin of pride. To transform ourselves and our society, to sustain us in that hard work, we must be grounded in something larger than our own egos. Ego will always fail us, because it is self-referential. It always asks the question, "How will my importance be raised up? What will I get out of this?" The way of the Spirit is different. It has to do with humility, with relinquishment. The question becomes, "What brokeness needs to be made whole? What am I called to give?"

As Unitarian Universalists, we should be at the center of the conversation about this new world. Why? Because we have the character and the courage and the values for this task. We are wise and passionate people. There is only one thing that can stop us: ourselves. When we pull back from the Sacred and act as if our faith were not central to our being. When we remain comfortable for too long, so that we cannot hear the cries of the forgotten. When we obsess about individual freedom and fail to bind ourselves in community, toward common purpose. When our religious communities concern themselves with the trivial and fail to focus on a mission larger than themselves and their needs.

I guess the big question is, why do all this anyway? Why not just plug in our own computers, stay behind locked doors, away from all these troubling things? We must act because it is only through resistance that we become clear, energized, truly alive. And it is when we are creating something new, together, that joy springs up within us and gives us hope and strength.

A new day is coming. I see it everywhere I look. Where will Unitarian Universalists stand? Let it not be said fifty years, a hundred years, from now, "Look what terrible injustice was being done—and the church, the church said nothing." Much has been given us, and much is required. Let us love mercy and do justice. Let us walk humbly with our God. Let our tradition be truly a living tradition. Else what can we say to the children when they ask us about the world we have given them? What can we say to the children?

EXCERPT FROM LETTER

NEW YORK *TIMES*, THE SUNDAY FOLLOWING THE ATTACKS OF SEPTEMBER 11, 2001

2001

There is the temptation, of course, to strike back with all our force, and soon—perhaps before we are entirely sure who is the enemy. That is the frustration we live with just now. I pray that we will not strike down innocent civilians, as our innocent civilians—accountants, office managers, secretaries—have been so cruelly struck down. Already there are beatings, harassment, destruction of property of our Arab-American and our Muslim neighbors. Somebody has to pay, we say. But let it not be those who have done no harm, whose only crime is having dark skin and a religion that is unfamiliar to us.

THE CHURCH AS A CIVIC INSTITUTION

PAPER PRESENTED AT REFUGIO, LA CASA DE MARIA
MONTECITO, CALIFORNIA
2002

We read the following words from Isaiah 61:

> The Spirit of God has sent us to bring good news to the oppressed,
> To bind up the brokenhearted,
> To proclaim liberty to the captives and release to the prisoners,
> To comfort all who mourn,
> To give them a garland instead of ashes,
> The oil of gladness instead of mourning,
> The mantle of praise instead of a faint spirit.
> They shall build up the ancient ruins,
> They shall raise up the former devastations,
> The devastations of many generations.
> You shall be named ministers of our God.

These words powerfully proclaim the mission of the church—but has the institutional church been faithful to that call? The record is decidedly spotty. This paper is grounded in the premise that the church is indeed called to be a witness to our public life, to transform civic life in keeping with the best understandings of the founders of our nation and with theological imperatives we hold in common—imperatives about how we are called to live together as a free and democratic people and yet as a people called to live in community, who wish to be faithful to a god of mercy, a god of love. Although I will allude to various religious groups, my focus will be on liberal mainline Protestant churches, of which Unitarian Universalist churches are the closest kin.

I will explore the institutional response of these churches to the moral challenges presented to them in the time of slavery and in the next century, during the era of the Civil Rights struggle and during the war in Vietnam. I will suggest the difficulties inherent in the institutional church's functioning both as a prophetic voice and also as a pastoral place of comfort and caring. Nonetheless, I believe that in spite of those dual purposes, which seem to conflict, the church is clearly and unequivocally called to function as a civic institution, contributing to the healing and transformation of a spiritually bankrupt society which increasingly gets its meaning from being a nation of obedient consumers. I believe there is no such thing as individual salvation, but only salvation within the context of community.

The conclusion of my paper suggests how the institutional church—should it choose to respect that call—could be more effective in the role of a civic institution, not only inviting a mature spirituality to individuals, but also transforming the societal context of their living, and the questionable pursuits of the nation, of which we are all citizens and for which we are therefore responsible.

Let's begin, shall we, with the Protestant Reformation, which was at least in part a human rights movement. Before the Reformation, there was one faith, one canon, one body of ecclesiastical law, and one set of accepted sacraments. Religious life was at one with political life. Luther, Calvin, and other early reformers all called for freedom from these given laws. If God has given all persons liberty to think and believe as they are led, without priestly intervention, then it follows that all must be free to practice these natural rights in other settings, as well. The Reformation, then, helped drive constitutional reforms during the years of democratic construction in the late 18th and 19th centuries.

Since many of the early settlers coming to the New World

came because of religious persecution, it follows that a passionately held goal was to create a society in which the state could not interfere with their religious lives. Their religious lives, however, dominated the state for a long while, and there was no separation of church and state.

Robert Bellah, the sociologist, speaks in his early book *The Broken Covenant*, about America's myth of origin. The Europeans who traveled to the New World were filled with hope: truly this was a land of virgin goodness and beauty, where they could begin again. The American myth was beautifully articulated by John Winthrop, the first leader of the Massachusetts Bay Colony, on board ship in 1630, even before landing in the New World. He said, in part, ". . . for wee must Consider that wee shall be as a Citty upon a Hill, the eies of all people are uppon us: soe that if wee shall deale falsely with our god in this worke we have undertaken and soe cause him to withdrawe his present help from us, wee shall shame the faces of many of gods worthy servants, and cause theire prayers to be turned into Cursses upon us till wee be consumed out of the good land whither wee are goeing." He compared the journey across the ocean to the crossing of the Red Sea, and he suggested that the Massachusetts Bay Colony was like the Promised Land. In other words, we are the chosen people, and we have a special role to carry out. (Bellah, *The Broken Covenant*, Chapter 1)

Our founding fathers were mostly not Christian, but they put forward a non-sectarian belief that God has blessed us and endowed us with special opportunity to do good. Our civic lives and our religious lives were indissolubly linked.

That sense of specialness has stayed with us, though we have little of the humility and religious piety of those early settlers. Rather, we have gone the way of imperialism, believing that we are superior beings, set apart not to serve God, but rather to dominate the known world, economically when we can and militarily when we have to, that our gospel of consumerism might be spread to the ends of the earth. "Go ye therefore into the world . . . ," to take and to sell. We have broken our covenant with God, and the consequences are unfolding.

In contrast to the French Revolution, where the Enlightenment was profoundly anti-religious, American civic life has always had a religious character. Early politicians drew upon philosophical principles of natural rights, but also the Bible for their arguments for liberty. Ministers were regular speakers at legislatures, civic celebrations, and patriotic holidays.

One of our own, Benjamin Rush, a signer of the Declaration of Independence, spoke these words: "The only foundation for a useful education in a republic is to be laid in religion. Without this there can be no virtue, and without virtue there can be no liberty, and liberty is the object and life of all republican governments." (Rush, "On the Mode of Education Proper in a Republic")

American oratory echoed, and still to some extent echoes, the cadence and color, of the pulpit. Abraham Lincoln was not a conventional Christian, but his speeches carry a deep theological import. Hear the echoes of his voice, which gave moral leadership to our country in perhaps the most difficult period of its history:

"Our reliance is in the love of liberty which God has planted in us."

"This nation, under God, shall have a new birth of freedom."

And listen to the Biblical cadences and allusions in Lincoln's Second Inaugural Address, as he speaks of the scourge of slavery: "Yet, if God wills that <this war> continue until all the wealth piled up by the bondsman's two hundred and fifty years of unrequited toil shall be sunk, and until every drop of blood drawn with the lash shall be paid by another drawn with the sword, as was said three thousand years ago, so still it must be said "the judgments of the Lord are true and righteous altogether." (Bellah, *The Broken Covenant*, p.54)

The greatest political orator of the last century, the Rev. Martin Luther King, Jr., was a Baptist minister, whose rhythms and rhymes and allusions came right out of the Old Testament. Though a less talented orator, Jesse Jackson uses similar cadences and allusions from the Bible. Another example is the stirring speeches of Senator Byrd of W. Virginia, protesting the invasion of Iraq.

Other politicians who may not have the rhetorical skill nevertheless maintain the connection between civic life and religion. Bill Clinton ended his speeches, "God bless you and God bless America." Jeb Bush, reelected governor of Florida, began his acceptance speech, "First of all, I want to thank almighty God."

The first amendment to the Constitution, which deals in part with the issue of the power of government over religion, reads "Congress shall make no law respecting an establishment of religion or prohibiting the free exercise thereof." This amendment protected religion from the state. Now the emphasis seems to be protecting the secular state from an overbearing influence of religion.

Stephen Carter, author of *The Culture of Disbelief*, says that we have unfortunately created a society that asks the religiously faithful to act in their public lives as if their faith does not matter to them. In our zeal to guard our public institutions against undue religious influence, we have encouraged people to split off their political and vocational lives from their spiritual lives. This unnatural split makes it all too easy for people to walk out the church door on Sunday and leave their religion behind until the following Sunday. (Carter, pp. 3-8) Much of our political rhetoric is dead language, with religion pulled out for use when a comforting sentiment is needed, and not really a genuine living contribution to public discourse.

The Liberal Protestant Church and Slavery

In the 19th century, we find churches and society at large beset with the dispute over slavery. Church leaders worried about conflict splitting their churches, and in particular Southern ministers felt the pressure to accede to the demands of their white parishioners. Their economic interests were at stake, of course, but it was more than that—their whole way of life, their whole way of seeing the world, their autonomy was at risk. Ministers, wanting to preserve the "peace," finessed the situation during the first half of the century by making their policy "non-interference in civil matters." But as things heated up, Southern whites, including church people, began to agitate about "outside intrusions." They insisted that their churches openly support slavery. Southern clergy began to justify secession, saying that the South was a sovereign government under siege. (Smith, pp. 1-2)

Churches divided themselves along the Mason Dixon line, with the Formalists (Congregationalists and Presbyterians), being the voices of moderation. Some, such as Lyman Beecher, gave leadership in the cause of abolition. The Antiformalists (Methodists, Baptist, and Christians) were from the middle and working classes, and they were in the forefront of opposition to the Formalists. They were anti-Yankee and anti-Republican. (Noll, pp. 151-2) Methodist minister William Wightman of South Carolina said, for example, that Christianity required obedience to civil laws for the sake of "social order, public peace, security and happiness. (Smith, p.6) But civil order is not always the realm of the Holy Spirit. The fact is that by 1844, at least 200 Methodist itinerant preachers owned 1,600 slaves, a thousand local preachers owned 10,000, and at least 25,000 Methodist laymen held more than 200,000 slaves. (Smith, quoting William Sweet, in Anne Loveland, *Southern Evangelicals and the Social Order,* p. 188)

Theologian Bill Jones has pointed out the need for power to legitimate itself, and so slaves were seen as less than human, so they would not have to be treated with the same rights and privileges of the whites. Scripture was used to support this perspective. Also there was a paternalism toward slaves, an ironic display of "Christian charity" which called for the white dominant class to take care of their slaves, who were thought unable to care for themselves. Some writers even went so far as to suggest that with slavery, there would be no unemployment for blacks.

Perhaps because women were victims of paternalism, too, they were leaders in the abolition movement, and their leadership was grounded in their religious faith. In 1833, when William Lloyd Garrison organized the American Anti-Slavery Society, Lucretia Mott and other female activists were invited to attend only as on-lookers. They formed the Philadelphia Female Anti-Slavery Society. Angelina Grimke, a member of the group, challenged women of the South to read the Bible and reflect upon the plight of the slaves. In addressing the Massachusetts State Legislature, she proclaimed: "I hold, Mr. Chairman, that American women have to do with this subject, not only because it is moral and religious, but because it is political, inasmuch as we are citizens of this republic and as such our honor, happiness, and well-being are bound up in its politics, government and laws."

It would be a mistake, of course, to believe that churches of the North were all hot-beds of abolition—quite the opposite. After all, New England was home to many of the cotton mills that profited from Southern agriculture. Most Unitarian churches, almost all of which were in the North, were "gradualists," who stressed patience, forbearance, and tolerance. Yes, slavery was bad, they said, but in time it will fade out. They mostly did not support the radicalism of William Lloyd Garrison or Theodore Parker. William Ellery Channing, a leading Unitarian minister, came rather late to the controversy, but grew more radical as he aged. Serving a congregation which included powerful men from the garment industry and who therefore needed the South's cotton, Channing was forbidden by his board to do a memorial service for the abolitionist Charles Follen. After that he preached less and less, and his ministry just faded out.

Late in the 19th century, with the rise of the factory system, there was a strong reform movement focused on such issues as child labor, unspeakable conditions in mental hospitals and prisons, education, and the work place. Most of the Unitarian efforts at reform, however, were the work of individuals, because of two reasons: (1) the distrust of authority and control, and (2) the long-held conviction that secular problems were not the domain of houses of worship. Tolerance of all positions made it difficult to unite church members to work toward one common goal.

Let us move now to the 20th century and focus on two moral issues that faced the church in contemporary times: the civil rights struggle and the war in Vietnam.

Church Activism During the Civil Rights Movement

Before 1963, most participation by white clergy in the civil rights movement was done by individuals or small groups. The Brown vs. the Board of Education decision had come nine years before, but churches had been content with passing resolutions. Little was done to eradicate discrimination. But the televised violence that they saw occurring in Birmingham was a wake-up call. (Friedland, *Lift Up*, p. 70)

Martin Luther King, Jr., knew what kind of violence he could expect in Birmingham from "Bull" Connor, and he chose that city to demonstrate to the whole nation how deep entrenched and violent racism was. The city fathers, anticipating the march, counseled against violence by segregationists and at the same time tried to minimize the pressure on authorities by black activists. Ten clergy leaders issued a statement professing sympathy for white Southern resentment but then stated that "defiance is <not> the solution." They urged that demands be brought peacefully to the courts. Like many clergy, they fell into a kind of passivity and piety that made their comments "unremarkable and ineffectual." (Friedland, *Lift Up*, pp.77-8) In response to the statement of these ten then, five white pastors from the Alabama Council on Human Relations risked their livelihoods—and indeed their lives—by joining four black ministers in issuing a public statement sympathetic to the demonstrations. Thirty-year-old Joseph W. Ellwanger, the white pastor of an all-black church (St. Paul's Lutheran), was the only white minister who took part in the demonstrations. (Friedland, *Lift Up*, p. 78)

Among white clergy, Robert MacAfee Brown and William Sloan Coffin were national leaders, but the Rev. Eugene Carson Blake and Rabbi Abraham Joshua Heschel took the first organizational steps in 1963. Heschel knew the pain of prejudice—he barely got out of Poland before the Nazis invaded, and they later murdered all of his family. "I am a brand plucked from the fire," he said. And speaking of racism, he said that even more insidious than that evil was indifference to evil, for that was "more universal, more contagious, more dangerous." On January 14 he delivered the keynote address to the National Conference on Religion and Race, where 657 clerical and lay representatives from 67 Protestant, Catholic, Jewish, and Greek Orthodox gathered. (Friedland, *Lift Up*, pp. 70-1)

Martin Luther King, Jr., reminded the audience that the church had been "content to mouth pious irrelevancies and sanctimonious trivialities," remaining "silent behind the anesthetizing security of stained-glass windows." If the church continued this way, King said, it would become "little more than an irrelevant social club." (Friedland, *Lift Up*, p. 73)

Episcopalian lay theologian William Stringfellow, a white lawyer from Harlem, said the conference was "too little, too late, and too lily-white." Only three speakers were black—others had been invited, but they had declined. Delegates, however, were determined to go forward, and they established the groundwork for similar conferences in other parts of the nation. They worked on lobbying, desegregating public accommodations in the South, held rallies, and worked for the passage of anti-discrimination ordinances. But the fact is that religious organizations never committed sufficient funds to the national organization, and it was forced to close down its New York office. (Friedland, *Lift Up*, pp. 74-6)

The clergy involved in the movement helped their congregations to see the issue as a moral one, and it was largely accepted as such in the East and Mid-West, where the black population was comparatively small. But when the whites were affected personally, the story was different. For example, northern clergy were harassed for challenging residential segregation. White mobs attacked civil rights marchers in Chicago, in some cases targeting white clergy and nuns. The Catholic Archdiocese then convinced the Southern Christian Leadership Conference not to go into the white suburbs. These were the same liberal Northerners who decried moderation and gradualism from the South. (Friedland, *Lift Up*, p. 141) Their colleagues in the South who courageously witnessed to the evils of discrimination were vilified by the unchurched and by church-goers as well. Perhaps these ministers were the true heroes among the white clergy.

The March on Washington for Jobs and Freedom was conceived of as black-organized and led; the presence of white liberal clergy and labor leaders lent support, but at the same time they pressured some of the more militant black leaders to tone down their rhetoric. The National Council of Churches contacted state councils of churches, asking them to take part. White leaders demanded that John Lewis, chair of Student Non-violent Coordinating Committee, omit phrases like "the masses" and "serious revolution." Lewis agreed, and the young militants in SNCC thought their leaders had sold out. (Friedland, *Lift Up*, pp. 85-7)

The March on Washington attracted somewhere between 200,000 and 300,000 participants, including 10,000 representatives from religious groups, led by 200 clergy. Despite the eloquence of many of the white speakers, they could not deny that they had come late to the scene. Most congregations in the Washington, D.C., area refused to endorse the march or provide lodging for participating clergy. (Friedland, *Lift Up*, pp. 88-9)

Churches have basically supported the status quo, in the arena of racial justice. Studies have shown that people affiliated with churches are no less racist than those who are not. In fact, those most involved in the life of their church are more prejudiced than those congregants less involved. Clergy responded to Martin Luther King, Jr.'s call to join him in Selma, where the march drew several thousand of them, but with few exceptions lay people were not there. (Hadden, p. 119) Some 1,500 Unitarian Universalists went to the March on Washington. Many others also went South to demonstrate.

White mainline churches face the problem that the clergy tend to be more ideologically committed than their flock. Church members seem willing to support charitable activities, but rarely sponsor political activity or protest against the state. They typically provide space for various social services, meal services, refugee programs, health care, and environmental improvement.

In 1965, only 7 percent of Protestant clergy said that they disapproved of Civil Rights, whereas 44 percent of the Protestant population disapproved. Two-thirds of clergy said they were sympathetic with the Civil Rights movement, but only one-third of the laity. Four-fifths of the laity compared to one-fifth of clergy agreed with the stereotype of the Negro as carefree, lazy, and irresponsible. (Hadden, p. 120) Those religious leaders who continued to call for open housing and fair employment practices were faced with a sharp drop in contributions from local churches. (Friedland, *Lift Up*, p. 141)

Despite the support given by church hierarchies, very few priests, ministers, and rabbis at the local parish level were willing to face hostile congregations and risk social ostracism, loss of their pulpits, or even physical violence. The most active white leaders in the movement were non-parish clergy less susceptible to lay pressure. (Friedland, *To Proclaim*, p. 13)

Church-goers are comfortable with charity, but not with justice. As the Brazilian Archbishop Com Helder Camara said long ago, "If I feed the poor, they call me a saint; if I ask why there are so many poor, they call me a Communist." It is telling that Martin Luther King, Jr., this great moral leader, was killed just as he was beginning to emphasize economic issues. At the time of his death he was organizing sanitation workers.

The kind of apathy to justice issues which we see displayed by most church-goers is a great barrier to a just society. For King, it was not the Klan or the citizens' councils that were "the greatest stumbling block in the stride toward freedom," but rather the moderates "more devoted to order than to justice." ("Letter from the Birmingham Jail," 1963, quoted by Friedland, *Lift Up*, p. 79) We will have to repent . . . , said King, "not merely for the vitriolic words and actions of the bad people . . . but for the appalling silence and indifference of the good people." ("Speech at the National Cathedral," Washington, D.C., 1968)

Church Activism During the Vietnam War

Vietnam was not on the radar screen of most Americans until July of 1965, when Johnson sent 50,000 additional troops. Until 1967 most Americans supported the President. Political activists in the pulpit were focused on racial discrimination as the most salient issue. Only doctrinaire pacifist groups such as the War Resisters League had protested, and their efforts were small and ineffective. (Friedland, *Lift Up*, p. 141)

Working against racism was an easier "sell" to churches than the war in Vietnam. Racism, justice and love were values that reflected the basic teachings of Judaism and Christianity and as such could be easily recognized and measured against the supposed ideals of our country. Clergy could appeal to Americans to live up to their principles of equality and democracy. (Friedland, *Lift Up*, p. 145)

The issues surrounding the Vietnam War were not so clear. Most Americans viewed the war as a political rather than a moral issue, and therefore speaking out against the war seemed an uncomfortable confluence between the church and the state—in spite of the fact that President Johnson turned to Cardinal

Spellman, the Archbishop of the Archdiocese of NY and to Billy Graham, to support the war. Those who protested found their patriotism questioned. Draft evaders were seen as traitors. Some activists understood that the war was racist. It was sapping funds from programs for the poor; black males were bearing the burden of the fighting, while privileged white males got deferments; and there were mounting casualties of Vietnamese, people of color. (Friedland, *Lift Up*, pp. 145-7)

The clergy were earlier to recognize the shaky basis for the war. After the first Buddhist monk set himself on fire in June of 1963 in a Saigon street, a group of 13 American clergymen, including Reinhold Niebuhr, Rabbi Julius Mark, and Episcopal Bishop James Pike, formed the Ministers' Vietnam Committee. They published full-page ads in the Washington *Post* and the New York *Times*, criticizing American support of the repressive regime in So. Vietnam. (Friedland, *Lift Up*, p. 142)

Robert McAfee Brown and William Sloan Coffin, through reading the paper and talking with their students, began to realize the unjust nature of the war. They also recognized the racist nature of the war. Some, though, who were active in racism work, would not join in the war protest—far fewer participated in the latter. Perhaps only 5 percent of the nation's clergy were actively opposed to the war, maybe 5 percent were supporters of the conflict, and most of the rest did not air their views readily in public. (Friedland, *Lift Up*, pp. 144-5)

Until the mid-1960's few clergy were willing to protest. In 1964, after the Gulf of Tonkin Resolution, the Washington Ministers' Association and the Council of Churches of Greater Washington circulated a petition calling upon Johnson to initiate a cease-fire and begin peace negotiations. Out of 750 clergy in Washington, only 105 agreed to sign. Ministers as well as lay people were uncertain, but felt that the experts in the White House and Pentagon must have known what they were doing. (Friedland, *Lift Up*, p. 143)

Martin Luther King, Jr., and Ralph Abernathy did not agree with Johnson, but did not want to alienate him and lose support for the civil rights movement, so protest was left to the white clergy. The leaders—Coffin, Brown, Heschel, and others—used church bureaucracies and mailing lists generated by the civil rights movement. Early in 1965 they established the Fellowship of Reconciliation. They submitted a full-page ad in the NYT asking Johnson to halt the bombing and call on all nations involved to launch an effort to heal and rebuild. Submitted to over 30,000 clergy, it was signed by around 3,000. (Friedland, *Lift Up*, pp. 148-9)

Clergy Concerned About Vietnam (CCAV) was convened by 100 leaders, including Rabbi Heschel and Richard Neuhous, on October 25, 1965. They decided to continue efforts as a formal group. This group was an important outlet for liberal religious leaders, who formed a national constituency. (Hall, p. 1)

The Berrigan brothers, Daniel and Philip, had long been activists in the civil rights movement. Daniel wanted to participate in the civil rights campaign in 1963, but his Jesuit superiors disapproved and sent him on sabbatical leave for a whole academic year to travel in Europe and Africa. Philip also managed to alienate his superiors when he gave a speech that included the words: "Do you honestly expect that we could so abuse our black citizens . . . so resist their moral and democratic rights, so mistreat . . . and murder them without all this showing up in our foreign policy?" He was transferred to an inner city parish in Baltimore two weeks later. (Friedland, *Lift Up*, p. 149)

Again, with the civil rights movement, the protest against the war in Vietnam showed clergy to be far more willing to question our policy than their congregants. In 1965 one thousand Catholic, Protestant and Jewish clergy took part in a silent demonstration, and a month later five hundred of them traveled to the Capital to lobby, but their efforts were to little avail, for they did not have the backing of their parishioners. (Friedland, *Lift Up*, p. 152)

David Halberstam said it well: the "best and the brightest"

were not evil people; they were liberals "committed to the good things in life, to decency and humane values . . . . <They were> urbane, modern, and if they were for a war, it would be a good war." (quoted by Friedland, *Lift Up*, pp. 153-4)

Difficulties in Finding a Prophetic Voice

So we can see that the churches' record as a prophetic voice, transforming the society of which it is a part, is spotty at best, then. Clergy, and even to a greater extent, laity have either ignored the cries of the oppressed or tried to mute their voices, or at worst been a vocal part of the oppression itself. There have been notable exceptions, of course, and these continue to inspire us with their courage.

What are the barriers to the liberal Protestant church in finding a prophetic voice and articulating a message of salvation beyond their own personal redemption? Why have we failed to show the clear and irrevocable connection between our own good and the good of the whole?

First, let's take a brief look at who *is* making the connection between religion and civic life, and why—what motivates their actions?

The Evangelicals

The traditionalists, or evangelicals, have been in recent years, as you know, organized and very active in politics, though their excesses have begun to discredit them with even very conservative political leaders. Their crucial role, as they see it, is in maintaining the moral order, protecting their version of religion, and addressing the breakdown of the traditional family. They seek to influence sexual mores ("just say no"), education (should be Christian, not secular), and foreign policy (don't give in to the godless Communists). They resisted the Social Gospel which took root at the end of the 19th century, and have emphasized personal salvation, rather than social justice. They believe that social problems are the result of individual moral failure.

What has made them so effective at grassroots mobilization? I believe they are motivated by fear of unsettling cultural changes, including the growing power of women and minorities. But it should be said that they know who they are, they know what they believe, and they know the identity of the enemy.

Here is the root, or core, difference setting them apart from liberals, who are awash in uncertainty. And there are lots of evangelicals: 11 percent of churches founded since 1970 describe themselves as liberal, 18 percent as moderate, and 69 percent as conservative or very conservative. Since early 1960 mainline denominations have been bleeding at the seams, losing members or showing no growth.

The Black Church

Black churches are as a rule very politically active. They are significantly more involved than white churches in partisan politics, voter registration drives, and campaigns to raise awareness of AIDS, for example. Congregants get political information and encouragement to act from their churches. (Cavendish, "Community Activism") The most visible manifestations are through black clergy, who act as a moral voice in many cities. The most prominent of these figures is Jesse Jackson, of course, who uses boycotts, demonstrations, and sit-ins to protest discrimination. Clergy are generally well supported by the black community, with 82 percent of African Americans saying that religion is a very significant force in their lives, and 80 percent saying they belong to a church. (Fowler, p. 157) Their liberation message is God's mercy to the poor and the captives, and God's judgment on those who misuse their power. This Christian message is clear, and provides a vision of a future they can move towards on this earth, not just the world beyond.

Still, all black churches are not alike, of course, and some—the Pentecostals, for example—are less accepting of political activity. Blacks are less sympathetic to gay rights and women's liberation than liberal whites, but studies show that blacks are more sympathetic than white evangelicals. (Fowler, p. 167)

Islamic movements have drawn a small number of blacks, their most gifted disciple being Malcolm X, who offered a challenge to Martin Luther King, Jr.'s doctrine of non-violent resistance. This movement emphasizes education, sexual discipline, hard work, cleanliness, and self-sufficiency. Louis Farrakhan now leads the Nation of Islam and is noted for his outbursts of rage and doctrine of separation. No one today can match the eloquence and passion of Martin Luther King, Jr., and Malcolm X.

The Catholic Church

The Roman Catholic Church has long had a commitment to ministries of social welfare, particularly in urban areas. Historically, they have provided services for immigrants, built hospitals and orphanages, and worked with the labor movement. In the 1960's the Church responded to racial unrest and poverty by introducing a multitude of new initiatives. Currently Catholics provide hands-on service and organize for justice work with interracial and ecumenical groups. They work in coalition with groups like the Industrial Areas Foundation and interfaith organizations. Both African American and Catholic churches openly confront the problems of urban life and have the infrastructure to support both social service and political action.

In Catholicism the message of social and economic justice is clear and is supported by the church hierarchy, most notably in the Pope's encyclicals. This decisive stance of the Catholic Church is in stark contrast to the liberal Protestant church, which is notably less confined to any authority except that of the local body. It is difficult for us to speak with one voice, or to carry the power of the body of a religious movement with a unified vision.

The Jews

Jews are very active politically and have an influence way beyond what their numbers might suggest. Except for the most religiously observant, they tend to be liberal: many are activists, they turn out the vote, and they give generously to political campaigns. They know that the left historically has been more favorable to minorities. At first Jews were very supportive of the civil rights movement and sent a disproportionately large number of students South to help with desegregation. But once the civil rights movement went North, the two communities began to divide over issues of black ownership of businesses, black leadership of public institutions, and affirmative action programs. These tensions led to black anti-Semitism and Jewish racism in two communities which, by all rights and logic, could have supported each other in their common experience of discrimination. (Fowler, pp. 310-13)

In the current conflict in the Middle East, Jews have exerted tremendously successful lobbying efforts with Congress and also with the media for support of Israeli policies in that area of the world.

Split Between Clergy and Laity in Liberal Mainline Churches

Most rank-and-file members of liberal Protestant churches have never supported the idea that the church should become intensely involved in public matters, believing that it is not the church's mission to provide leadership on race, poverty, and peace. When clergy began to speak out in the 1960's, conflicts emerged, and the costs were high. Activists reported that their churches lost members and financial support as a result of social justice activities. Many clergy were censured by their church's board, and some lost their positions. (Quinley, "The Dilemma of an Activist Church" p. 7) As many as 67 clergy in Unitarian Universalist churches had negotiated resignations during the Vietnam war years. (According to activist minister Paul Sawyer.)

During the years of the war, many more clergy were dovish than the general public, or their parishioners. A study done in 1968 of 1,580 Protestant parishes in California showed that 57 percent of the clergy supported a halt to the bombing, whereas only 21 percent of the American people did. (Friedland, *To Proclaim*, p. 9) Local parishioners were more than twice as likely to discourage a minister's anti-war activities, as they were to encourage him. One in ten of activist ministers reported an organized effort to have him removed from the pulpit. (Hadden, p. 126)

Members of mainline churches are comfortable with providing acts of charity and philanthropy, like providing food or tutoring poor children, or finding shelter for the homeless. As one woman responded in a survey, "Doing things for people where there is someone hurting. That's where the church belongs. . . . . I'm disturbed when the pastor starts talking politically and yet sometimes I see that . . . . I believe in the total separation of church and state."

From the perspective of the laity, the church or synagogue should act as a sanctuary from the pressures of the outside world. The flight to the suburbs, another sanctuary where church members are socially and economically and racially similar, contributes to this attitude of indifference to the plight of those unfortunate ones who wander the central city in need of shelter and food. Surveys show that lay people—82 percent of Protestants, at least—believe that "clergy have a responsibility to speak out as the moral conscience of this nation." However, they are comfortable with general abstractions, not specific social problems. Clergy are pressured to conform to the "values and norms of the groups they lead." (Friedland, *To Proclaim*, p. 8) Scholar Jeffrey Hadden puts it this way: ". . . the church has permitted people to sit in comfortable pews and reaffirm belief in brotherhood and love while escaping the implications and applications of this belief . . . . churches have compromised their vision to more palatable charity bazaars and supper for the far-away pagans and orphans." (Hadden, p. 122)

The '60's were years of revolution and social change; but in the '70's churches have given more attention to traditional religious issues and the development of personal spirituality. Congregants turned inward for answers. But self-improvement goes only so far. Losing membership and public trust, churches have been concerned more with institutional self-preservation and are unwilling to antagonize those who fill the collection plate. The "New Breed" of activists, as Harvey Cox referred to them in the '60's, was never more than a minority force in a largely conservative tradition. (Fowler, p. 301) This situation is nothing less than tragic, considering that clergy and the church represent the sacred, in a secular world. Lending sacred power to the misuse of human power is like giving political authority the authority of God, which is a travesty of our role. Says Peter Berger in his classic work, *The Sacred Canopy*, "When the socially defined reality has come to be identified with the ultimate reality . . . then its denial takes on the quality of evil." (Berger, pp. 33-4)

Mainline Protestant churches have become increasingly secularized and have begun to compete with secular organizations for attention. The concept of sin, and therefore moral responsibility, has been replaced with therapy. Church organizational development has descended into calling parishioners "customers" and asking how we can please our customers. Many churches have become mere "service providers." Sociologist Robert Bellah speaks of this trend as "religious commodification." He cites an example from a suburban newspaper in the San Francisco Bay area: "The members of St. John's Lutheran Church have a money-back guarantee. They can donate to the church for 90 days, then if they think they made a mistake, or did not receive a blessing, they can have their money back. The program is called 'God's Guarantee' and the pastor is confident it will work." (Bellah, *The Good Society*, pp. 93-4) We have no coherent message, as do the evangelicals. Our moral relativism keeps us from having a clear mission and a clear voice.

Why the Church Must Move from Charity to Justice

Subsequent to the election of Ronald Reagan as President in 1982, the institutions in the United States that have garnered overweening power have been business and the government. Because of increasingly expensive political races paid for by wealthy constituents and companies, money seems to rule our political life these days. It remains to be seen how much effect our recent movement toward campaign finance reform will affect our electoral system. We have a government largely by the rich and for the rich.

How will reform come then? How will justice be done? How will power come to be shared? Change, I believe, will not come chiefly through government or business, but through what is sometimes called the "third sector"—churches, schools, non-profits, labor unions. These are mediating institutions, standing at the intersections between public and private life. Churches are unique in that they, more than any other of these institutions, provide a liberating message through time, by tradition and scripture. It is here and only here, among institutions in our society, that we learn that we are part of something larger than ourselves—part of the working of God through history—and understand that that something will continue long after we are gone. We do not have to be attached to the fruits of our work; we have only to be faithful. It is in the grounding of our work in faith, then, that sustains us through harsh conditions, bitter criticism. Our tenacity is born from a profound understanding that we are partners with the Spirit in redeeming a hurting world. Therein lies our uniqueness.

It's time for us to use our formidable power—formidable if it is harnessed to righteous purpose—to move from charity to justice. Else how are people of faith any different from the fancy dressers at charity balls pictured in local newspapers? The problem with charity is that it is a one-down, Lady Bountiful approach: "Out of my largess, I'm going to bestow a tiny portion onto you. Not that you deserve it, mind you, but because I have a good heart. I am a good person. My laudable works prove that I am." Such an approach skirts questions of power. No power is shared, and there is no threat to the one who gives. The giver absolutely controls what and how the gift is given. There is a place for charity, and that is two-fold: (1) to give emergency aid and (2) to allow comfortable middle-class people to have some contact with persons in need. Perhaps some of these middle-class church-goers will not stop at charity, but will begin to ask why so many people suffer in a rich society such as ours.

Most of us in white liberal churches are well-educated and relatively sophisticated professionals—successful, it might be said. But theologian James Luther Adams has this to say about the religion of comfortable people: "This religion of the successful amounts to a systematic concealment of and separation from reality—a hiding of the plight of those who in one sense or another live across the tracks. In the end this concealment comes from a failure to identify correctly and to enter into combat with what St. Paul called 'the principalities and powers of evil.' The religion of the successful turns out then to be a sham spirituality, a cultivated blindness, for it tends to reduce itself to personal kindliness and philanthropy costing little. Thus it betrays the world with a kiss." (Adams, p. 83)

I wonder if we are not still under the sway of the Protestant Ethic, which promised that if we worked hard we would be rewarded—in this world and in the next, as well. The great majority of people in this culture seem to believe that poverty is a moral problem, rather than an economic one. The poor are poor because they are lazy. We would never dare articulate this point of view in our liberal churches, but I wonder how deeply ingrained this social perspective is.

The former President Bush talked glowingly of "a thousand points of light," and his son proposes that churches enter into a partnership with the government in providing services for the poor. He wants us to busy ourselves with food programs for hungry people whom he and his policies have abandoned. He wants us to tutor children who have no homes. He wants us to provide day care for the children of parents who must work two jobs to survive. In short, he wants us to substitute for the social work agencies whose budgets have been cut and cut and cut. He wants us to solve the social problems created by a shameful distribution of wealth in this country. But churches do not have the capacity—the financial or human resources—to take on the vast social and economic problems of our country. Neither can churches plan comprehensively, so that money doesn't go just to the most appealing projects—it's easier to raise money for children with disabilities than for prostitutes who wish to leave their profession, for example.

It's not that there is never a place for hands-on work, for it is often here that a volunteer falls into a new consciousness, an indignation at the suffering of others, and decides to work for systemic change—or at least support others who do. After a few months at the soup kitchen, a church volunteer may begin to ask Dom Helder Camara's question, "Why are there so many hungry people?" And why, though I work hard in this soup kitchen, does the line of hungry people grow longer and longer? I'm not saying, either, that we should stop giving donations to charities and funnel all our expendable funds into political action. Giving donations to the local food bank is important, because today, right now, people are hungry. Oregon has more hunger, in fact, that any other state in the union. But food banks are emergency measures—we can't stop there. We must look at how poverty and racism are institutionalized and therefore continue unabated under the eyes of good, compassionate folks in the pews of our churches.

We have seen critical points in our nation's history in which some churches, and some church movements, have acted prophetically: the Quakers on abolition and on peace; the mainline liberal clergy who supported the civil rights movement; the black church as it works for economic reform through education and voter registration. We need to do more of this transformative work more of the time. Our calling is not to be a part of the system, but to be an external critic and an alternative voice, imagining and articulating the kind of world that is possible and inviting others to move towards that alternative. We need to be courageous enough to rattle some cages. We need to move from the liberal tendency to just tweak the status quo enough to make us feel comfortable, to the more radical (meaning, *from the root*) approach of genuinely sharing power.

We Unitarian Universalists like to think of ourselves as justice-seeking, but we are seriously hampered by our character and by our organization, or rather our lack of it. We have a loyalty to individualism and a distrust of authority; therefore, we do not have a unity of purpose. We fear the power of the clergy, so we hold them in check whenever possible, to keep them from leading boldly and speaking a truth that might not be our own truth. Too many of our churches and fellowships have no discernible vision or mission—they exist to please themselves, as any social or civic club might. A more radical social and political thrust is belied by establishment values.

How Can We Answer Our Call, as People of Faith?

Of course in the United States there exists a great plurality of faiths. At the founding of our country, whatever common religion we shared, it was some version of Protestant Christianity. Puritan culture dominated American life through the 19th century. But today we have Judaism, Islam, Buddhism—we are no longer a "Christian nation," and we must allow a diversity of expression. But the Constitutional separation of church and state does not mean that religious faith and values should be absent from public discourse. (Olliff, "Religion and Public Life," p. 7, referencing Thiemann)

The most significant religious contributions to American public life have come from two sources, (1) black churches and (2) post-Vatican II Roman Catholicism, says Ken Olliff. Both groups have a theological context which undergirds their faith and suggests a direction for an expression of that faith in the larger community. In other words, they know who they are and what they stand for.

Olliff says of liberals that those "communities that are undergoing a perpetual identity crisis do not make for interesting conversation partners." (Olliff, p. 8, quoting Thiemann) Nor will these churches, I might add, attract many followers, since they cannot say to those wandering in the thicket of spiritual confusion, just who they are and what they stand for.

As Unitarian Universalists, we might take heed to his words. How can we answer our call, as people of faith, in this day of pluralism, even as we invite that pluralism in our own tradition? We are called to witness, yes, we would agree to that—but from what ground do we witness? Perhaps the first step is to articulate who we are and what we are about. What is our core? What are the values that hold us together?

Certainly we know that we believe that the Kingdom of God must be created on this earth, rather than the next. Given that commitment, we can start there with our justice work, for surely common goals emerge, like genuine democracy, peace, egalitarianism, sharing of resources, and protecting the earth, our home.

We are fond of making grand resolutions and not backing them up with resources. We need to fund our dreams, and we need to think wisely about how our money is spent in this Association and in our local churches. What is the pay-off for the money spent? Why don't more of our churches, in particular our large churches, have social justice directors on staff? We need to educate, train, and organize. We need to work in coalitions with other groups in the community that have similar goals. A paid staff person enhances a church's capability tremendously.

We need to inform and to encourage learning beyond the messages from the corporate media. One of the findings of James Kubal-Komoto, a minister in our movement who has done research in the area of justice work, is that the single most important factor in developing justice work is adult religious education programs, which not only inform, but also give participants support. Participation builds social capital.

We must always be grounded in the Spirit, in something larger than ourselves. The vertical dimension must be addressed, not just the horizontal dimension of our faith. Our grounding must come from the Source of our strength and must not be generated from egotism and self-righteous condemnation, which all too often lead to a projection of our own guilt and negligence onto others.

The leadership of the clergy in justice work cannot be overemphasized. And clergy cannot lead without knowledge of American culture, politics, and economic theory and practice. Our seminaries should take it upon themselves to include this subject matter in their curricula, and settled ministers should be given time and resources from the UUMA and from the UUA, should they feel they need to deepen their knowledge in this arena.

Ministers are called as priest and as prophet, roles which are difficult to reconcile at times. They are responsible for keeping their institutions as stable as possible, so that conflict doesn't tear them apart or dissipate their energies. I believe that the love of the pastor for the people and a strong emphasis on pastoral care will lay the groundwork for the minister's speaking out boldly on issues. If congregants know their minister loves them, they will be more likely to be open to a prophetic message. Having said that, though, I believe that the minister must discern where the bulk of the congregants are, and take them a little further, pushing the edge as far out as possible.

I believe it's crucial for the minister to speak out clearly and boldly and to avoid wishy-washy attempts at inclusivity, as in "some people think this, other people think that." Congregants need to know that they can, and are expected to, differ with their minister, and that they will be respectfully listened to. But the minister's speaking out with integrity and power will encourage congregants to find their own strength, their own voices. Passivity in a minister is not respected, and will encourage confusion and insecurity among congregants. It is inevitable, of course, that some congregants will be distressed because of a strong justice message from the minister, and some—and these tend to be the larger donors—may object and even leave the church. But so be it. We are not called, as Jesus said, that we might be comfortable—we are called that we might be free.

Living the Parable

Wanting to be helpful, we all
see ourselves as the Samaritan
rather an the priest or his assistant,
and never as the bruised man in the ditch,
stripped and penniless, taken
to a room smelling of figs and tallow,
where he turns painfully in bed,
tonguing his chipped tooth,
touching his swollen eye.
After all, who would imagine himself
mugged somewhere between Jerusalem and
Jericho
when he could ride in like some minor deity
on a donkey packed with oil and wine,
his fat purse tucked away, credit unlimited?

Better to be the one without cracked ribs,
safe on the hard-packed road,
pausing long enough to help
some creature with no luck—
a dog, a sheep, a beaten man—
not one of us.

—Neal Bowers

Herein lies the lesson for a religious people motivated by noble sentiments, but tethered to the pole of privilege, wanting the transformation of self and of church, but wanting more, approval and comfort and security, not as God grants these, but as this world grants them. From our self-righteousness comes alienation. In our fierce sense of individualism, we do not realize that we cannot be saved alone. The problem is, this world passes away, and the great leveler, Death, puts us at last with our brothers and sisters.

Bibliography

Note: Unfortunately, I have lost my original bibliographical information for this paper. As much as possible, I've tried to recreate my sources.

Adams, James Luther. *The Prophethood of All Believers*, ed. George Beach, Beacon Press, 1986.

Bellah, Robert, *The Broken Covenant: American Civil Religion in Time of Trial*, Seabury Press, 1975.

________, et al. *The Good Society*, First Vintage Books, 1992.

Berger, Peter, *The Sacred Canopy: Elements of a Sociological Theory of Religion*, Doubleday, 1967.

Camera, Dom Helder. *Dom Helder Camera: Essential Writings*, Orbis Books, 2009.

Carter, Stephen L., *The Culture of Disbelief: How American Law and Politics Trivialize Religion*, Basic Books, 1993.

Cavendish, James C., "Community Activism: a Comparison of Black and White Congregations," *Journal for the Scientific Study of Religion*, September 2000, pp. 371-384.

Fowler, Robert Booth, *Unconventional Partners: Religion and American Liberal Culture*, Erdman Publishing Company, 1989.

Friedland, Michael B., *Lift Up Your Voice Like a Trumpet: White Clergy and the Civil Rights and Antiwar Movements, 1954-1973*, University of North Carolina Press, 1998.

________. *To Proclaim the Acceptable Year of the Lord: Social Activism and Ecumenical Cooperation Among White Clergy in the Civil Rights and Antiwar Movements of the 1950's and 1960's*, Ph. D. Thesis, University Microfilms, Boston College Leaves 710-750, 1993.

Hadden, Jeffrey K., *The Gathering Storm in the Churches: the Widening Gap Between Clergy and Laymen*, Doubleday, 1969.

Hall, Mitchell K. *Because of Their Faith: Calcav and Religious Opposition to the Vietnam War*, Columbia University Press, 1990.

Jones, William R., *Is God a White Racist?: A Preamble to Black Theology*, Anchor Press, 1973. Reprinted by Beacon Press, 1997.

King, Martin Luther Jr. "Remaining Awake Through a Great Revolution," sermon at Washington National Cathedral, March 31, 1968, collected in *A Testament of Hope: The Essential Writings and Speeches of Martin Luther King, Jr.*, ed. James Melvin, HarperCollins, 1986, pp. 268-78.

Loveland, Anne, *Southern Evangelicals and the Social Order, 1800-1860*, Louisiana State University Press, 1980.

Noll, Mark A., *The Civil War as a Theological Crisis*, University of North Carolina Press, 2006. Reprinted 2015.

Olliff, Ken A., Th.D. Seminar Paper, "Reconstructing Theological Liberalism," Harvard Theological School, Dec. 15, 2000.

Rush, Benjamin. "On the Mode of Education Proper in a

Republic," collected in *Essays Literary, Moral & Philosophical*, printed by Samuel F. Bradford, 1798.

Smith, H. Shelton. *In His Image, But . . . Racism in Southern Religion*, Duke University Press, 1972.

Thiemann, Ronald. *Constructing a Public Theology: the Church in a Pluralistic Culture*, Westminster/John Knox Press, 1991.

________. *Religion and Public Life: a Dilemma for Democracy*, Georgetown University Press, 1996.

Quinley, Harold E., "The Dilemma of an Activist Church: Protestant Religion in the Sixties and Seventies," *Journal for the Scientific Study of Religion*, Vol. 13, No. 1, March 1974, pp. 1-21.

________. *The Prophetic Clergy: Social Activism Among Protestant Ministers*, Wiley, 1974.

________. "The Protestant Clergy and the War in Vietnam," *The Public Opinion Quarterly*, Vol. 34, No.1, Spring 1970, pp. 43-52.

CALLED TO SERVE

ADDRESS TO NEW GRADUATES
MEADVILLE LOMBARD SEMINARY
2004

Let me begin by saying thank you! I am pleased and greatly honored to have been given an honorary doctorate from Meadville-Lombard, and then honored once again to be asked to speak at this auspicious occasion.

I want to speak this afternoon particularly to the graduates, and even more particularly to the ones of you who are planning to become parish ministers, since that is what I feel most qualified to speak on, having been in the trenches now for some years. I had some difficulty in deciding what to title my address today. I first thought to title it "What Nobody Ever Tells You in Seminary" or, alternatively, "Get Out While You Still Can."

I'm assuming that you graduates going into ministerial service are doing so because you believe you have been "called"—but what a confusing, amorphous word that can be. Personally, I had a lot of trouble with this concept of call. I had doubts all the way through seminary. I had doubts as I went through my Ph.D. program. I certainly had doubts when I was pre-candidating—and for those of you who don't know, pre-candidating is the extensive interview—two and a half days—that a minister does with a prospective church. I did an unprecedented ten pre-candidating interviews over a period of two years—five each year—and by the time I got to Portland, OR, number ten, I was frankly doubting whether or not I was supposed to be a minister. Oh, I was getting offers, all right—but nothing felt right—nothing felt like a call. I wondered, "Why did I spend eight years in school? Surely there must have been some purpose to all of this." But when I arrived in Portland, I knew almost immediately that this was the church I was supposed to serve. I told the search committee that during my first interview. I said, "This is where I'm called to be." Well, they coughed a lot. And it took them two more months to come to the same conclusion. But I had this interior knowing—against all logic of course, for this was my first church—I had this quiet sense that Portland was where I was supposed to be.

So my first piece of free advice—and it's worth every penny—is that a call is real. A call to ministry is real and a call to a specific church is real, and you will know it not because of logic, not because of geography or salary or prestige or anything else, except that your heart will lead you there, and you cannot easily turn away. Now I'm not saying you shouldn't do your homework—you should find out everything you can from everybody you can about any church you're considering. But in the end, it is your heart that will tell you where you are supposed to be. And if that match is good, chances are you will flourish and the church will flourish.

One of my titles was "Get Out While You Still Can." That reminds me of the crisis I had just before I was to be ordained. About two weeks before the date, I had a stole made for the ordination service—a long shiny thing with lots of gold Coptic crosses, made by an order of nuns. As I drove away from the nunnery, it hit me: crosses, sacrifice! *What* am I doing? What I had in mind was a little power, not sacrifice, not servanthood. Whoa! Furthermore, I'm going to have to be good from now on. No, really good. Exemplary. Furthermore, this deal is for life. Once I'm ordained, I'll always be a minister. I can't divorce ordination. That's when the real doubt set in. *I am not good enough,* I said to myself. *I cannot go through with the ordination.* I wasn't talking about skills, I was talking about moral virtue. I was not good enough.

In a panic, I went to talk to Gordon McKeeman, who was then the Acting President of Starr King School. I tearfully told him of my dilemma, and he looked at me and said the one thing I needed to hear, to make me stop shaking inside. He said, "Remember that the efficacy of the sacrament does not depend upon the purity of the celebrant." Oh. I was to be a part of something bigger than myself. Something good and true was to be working through me. I did not have to depend on my frail flesh to carry the day. I would try, I would do my best. But I did not have to be perfect. I had a partner, and that partner was the Holy, and I just needed to be a willing conduit.

The truth is that I'm frightened every time I get up to preach, whether I'm preaching to twelve or to twelve hundred. It is daunting to consider speaking to other souls about the deepest concerns of their hearts. It is an awesome responsibility. *What are you doing up here?* And so I always have to remind myself that I never do this work alone. I do my very best, and I always think it's not enough, and yet through grace it becomes enough.

WILL THE REAL JESUS PLEASE STAND UP?

KEYNOTE ADDRESS AT CONFERENCE "NEW WINE IN OLD WINESKINS," MULTNOMAH BIBLE COLLEGE
PORTLAND, OREGON
2005

I want to begin by thanking Dr. Metzger for organizing this conference—I know my congregants, as well as my colleagues in ministry have been asking, "How do we bridge the cultural divide?" It seems to be so great. I myself have struggled with this talk. In fact, I woke in the middle of the night on two separate occasions, to find myself thinking about this speech, unable to go back to sleep. Each time I got up and wrote a speech, then tore it up. This is my third attempt.

In a very real sense, I am one of you—I am a Christian, with an interesting faith journey. I was raised Roman Catholic, but at the age of twelve or so, I found that I was having difficulty with some of the dogma of the Catholic church, like transubstantiation and confession. Also, the priest told me that I couldn't read and interpret the Bible for myself. I guess I was a Protestant from the beginning. So I decided I had to leave the church. The priest came to my home, then, to talk with me. I remember that he sat on one end of the sofa, and I sat on the other, and he looked at me, and he said, "Marilyn Jane," (you know, in the South we have those double names) he said, "Marilyn Jane, you are going to hell if you don't return to the Catholic Church."

So I asked him, "Father, do you believe that God knows everything?"

"Yes, my child," he said.

"Then God would know that I don't really believe, so even if I came back to the Church, it wouldn't do me any good." He left that day, feeling that another soul had slipped away.

Now my grandparents, with whom I was living, were Southern Baptists, and so I started attending their church. No sooner than I did, though, I was told that Catholics were not Christians, and that unless I gave my life to Jesus on Baptist terms—yes, you guessed it—I was going to hell.

Well, I did accept Jesus as my savior, as they said, when I was fourteen. I remember the night. It was at a revival led by Angel Martinez, who was about the best looking man I had ever seen. When he gave the altar call, I looked into his dark eyes, and I just went on down the aisle and put my hand in his. "Yes, Angel, I've come home to Jesus."

I remained a Southern Baptist as an adult, and my husband and I and our two young children attended a large Baptist church in Lexington, KY. But then the marriage went bad. I did everything I could to avoid getting a divorce, because that was the last thing I wanted to do—I talked with our pastor, we went to a series of counselors, I prayed about it—but finally I did decide to divorce. I felt it was a Spirit-led decision. But the Baptist church didn't see it that way. Our friends there deserted us. And I was told that I could no longer teach the children. I think I was considered a fallen woman.

I remember weeping in my therapist's office one day, telling her how I had lost my whole social structure, telling her how lonely I was, and she said, "Why don't you go over to the Unitarian Universalist Church? There are lots of divorced people over there." I did go, and there were lots of divorced people, yes, but also lots of all kinds of people—the important thing is that I was accepted as I was, and I had a place where I was loved and nurtured, and could give my gifts. I became a leader there—whereas in the Baptist Church, I couldn't even become a Deacon, because I am a woman.

I also think the manner in which I was brought into the Unitarian Universalist church is significant. The first time I went, it was not to church, but to a volleyball game on Friday night. I was sitting there on the sidelines, not knowing anyone, too shy to jump up and take a spot when a game was over. Finally someone reached a hand down to me and said, "Don't you want to play?" I said, "Yes," and he pulled me up, up into the game and I was part of the group after that. His name was Titus, and he was a black man. I had been a Christian all my life, and I had never been in church with a black person. What's wrong with this picture?

I still consider myself a Christian—a Unitarian Universalist Christian: *Unitarian* meaning "God is one," and *Universalist* meaning "universal salvation, all are saved." (Note that we are not Unity church, nor are we the Unification church—we have Christian roots, having come out of the left wing of the Protestant Reformation. Unitarians and Universalists, similar in theology, came together as one in 1961.) The Christian faith itself could potentially be a huge unifying element in this country, where 85 percent of our people consider themselves Christian—in fact, we call ourselves "a Christian Nation."* When I thought about what to say to you today, about what we have in common, I realized that we have Jesus in common. I love Jesus, and you love Jesus.

But the question I want to put before us today is, "Who is this Jesus we profess to follow?" In order to prepare for this talk, I went back through the gospels, just to refresh my memory, and this is what I found:

Jesus said over and over and over again—love is the answer, love is the way. Time after time the scribes and pharisees tried to

* It should be noted that Christianity, Judaism, and Islam are all Abrahamic faiths, and if only by that common ancestry, have a basis for relationship and rich conversation among their adherents.

trap him into violating the law, because they were afraid of his power—his power coming from God, whereas they had only the authority of their outdated rules and their position as religious leaders. And Jesus kept saying, "Your rules are worthless, the only law is the law of love." You know the scripture. These religious authorities were watching to see if Jesus healed the man with the withered hand on the Sabbath. And Jesus said to them, "Is it lawful to do good on the Sabbath or to do evil? Is it lawful to save a life?" And then the scripture says (Mark, Ch. 3): "He looked round about on them with anger, being grieved for the hardness of their hearts."

Again, in Matthew, Ch. 5, we read the words of Jesus: "Ye have heard that it hath been said, An eye for an eye, and a tooth for a tooth, but I say unto you, turn the other cheek—love your enemies, bless them that curse you"—whoa, that's the radical message of Jesus! LOVE TRUMPS EVERY LAW, EVERY RULE—YOU MEASURE EVERYTHING BY THE PRINCIPLE OF LOVE—don't look in the scripture, don't go by your traditions, throw your rationalizations out the window—go straight to the heart. What does your heart say, what does love demand? That's the Jesus I see in Matthew, Mark, Luke and John.

Jesus turns everything upside down—all our normal expectations. For example, we believe that those who work hard can expect to be prosperous—right? That may be a cultural ethic in the United States, but that's not what Jesus said. He said, "Lay not up for yourselves treasures upon earth, where moth and dust doth corrupt . . . . But lay up for yourselves treasures in heaven, for where your treasure is, there will your heart be also." (Matthew, Ch. 6)

The rich young ruler comes to Jesus and asks, "Good Master, what good thing shall I do, that I may have eternal life?" (Matthew, Ch. 19) Jesus says, keep the commandments. He says, well I've done that. Well, only one thing more, says Jesus—sell all you have and give the money to the poor. Now I don't believe Jesus meant that literally—but I do believe that he was telling this fellow that following the rules was not enough—you have to give *yourself* away—don't be coming here pre-occupied with your own salvation—don't you get it? It's not about you, Jesus is saying, it's about others.

That emphasis couldn't be clearer than it is in Matthew 25, when Jesus says, essentially, "When you die, there's going to be a test." Did you feed the hungry? Did you shelter the stranger? Did you take care of the sick, and visit those in prison?

So I'm reading the scripture, and I'm thinking, "We're a Christian nation? I don't think so!" Nearly 18 percent of American children lived in poverty last year. The U.S. Department of Agriculture reported last year that the number of households that were "food insecure with hunger" had climbed more than 26 percent between 1999 and 2003—and Oregon is one of the states with the most hunger. We are the most violent of the developed countries in the world, with a murder rate four or five times that of countries in Europe. We have six or seven times as many of our citizens in prison. We're the only Western democracy left that executes its citizens—mostly in states that are Christian strongholds. Not to mention our militarism—which most recently has cost tens of thousands of Iraqi and now two thousand American lives. A Christian nation? I think not, by these measures. I believe Jesus said: "He who lives by the sword will die by the sword." (Matt. 26:52)

So with the situation in this country being what it is, in terms of poverty, hunger, racism, and violence, what do I see Christians in the popular culture overwhelmingly focusing on? The end-time. And churches preaching the gospel of prosperity—how you can get yours. Churches calling people to be better consumers, to improve themselves, to get better self-esteem. Jesus's radical message focused on others, not on ourselves. Politically, the focus for Christians is on two sexual issues, issues to do with the body: abortion and homosexuality—women, this is what you must do with your body, never mind the circumstances; gays and lesbians and bisexuals and transgender folks, there is only one way to love, and it's our way. What do you think Jesus would say about that? What would the law of love call us to do? If nothing, Jesus was inclusive. He ate with tax collectors, the very people who were persecuting his people. He was friendly with prostitutes.

I've got to tell you that I had a lot of pain when I arrived here in Portland fourteen years ago and saw that Christians were leading the assault against the civil rights of gays and lesbians, of whom I have many in my church. Sometimes they would come through the line after a sermon and weep in my arms, with fear, trying to live in that atmosphere of hate. And of course so much violence was being done then and still is done now to gay men, in particular. I think of Matthew Shepherd there in Laramie, Wyoming, strung up on a fence and left to die, a victim of this kind of hate. There are no finer people in my church than my gay and lesbian folks—and when they hurt, I hurt. I *hurt*.

It is distressing to me as well that Christians don't seem so concerned about policies that further reward the very rich and further impoverish the poor. Oh, a little charity here and there is a good thing—a soup kitchen is good—but how about asking why there are so many hungry people—right here in Multnomah County? What about worrying less about individual sin and working against systemic evil? I see Christians—and this is in my denomination as well as in others—being comfortable with charity, but not so comfortable with justice. What did the prophet say? "Let justice roll down like waters, and righteousness like an ever-flowing stream." (Amos 5)

So, how to bridge this cultural divide? I think it is a cultural divide, and not truly a religious one—there would be a lot more unity if those of us who count ourselves as Christian would actually attempt to follow Jesus. We need to bring our theology in line with what the scripture says, not what would be easy or what would feel good for us. If our theology pulls us away from Jesus' radical message about helping the poor and the weak and the disenfranchised, then we need to question our theology. The dominant theologies of Christianity today—I have to say, the exception is the Black church—don't have much to do with the Jesus of the scriptures.

As people who claim to follow Jesus, we need to ask ourselves, the single question that Jesus asked folks over and over again, "What does *love* demand of us?" Not what does our pastor say. Not what do our political leaders say. Not what do the neighbors think. Just that one question: "What does *love* demand of us?" If we try to answer that question together, as human beings, if we really asked ourselves, "What would Jesus do?" we might not agree on everything, but perhaps we will begin to tear down the golden calves we have erected—our cultural idols to prosperity, to American domination, to violence, and to the rule-making and its self-righteousness that keeps us separate and apart from our sisters and brothers. We need one another, and the world needs Christians who truly wish to follow Jesus, however imperfectly we may do it—and I confess I do it very imperfectly— but we need to truly try to follow this revolutionary and his radical rule of love.

Francis David was one of our earliest theologians and a martyr to our Unitarian faith. He said, "We need not think alike to love alike." I hope we can go forward together in that spirit.

OPENING REMARKS FOR CHALICE LIGHTING

UNITARIAN UNIVERSALIST GENERAL ASSEMBLY
PORTLAND, OREGON
2007

And now as we begin the worship segment of our time together, we light our chalice, a fitting symbol for a people who have stood for hundreds of years for freedom of belief, for openness to new revelation, and for the power of love to transform the world.

You have come to Oregon, to the West Coast, to the final stop of the Lewis and Clark expedition—you have come to the end of the frontier. As a nation we have come to the end of a frontier of sorts—a nation that promised always better, always more —that promised a chicken in every pot, that promised trickle-down, that promised that each generation would be more prosperous than the one before. That frontier of rising consumerism is dead—its time has come and gone, for it is absolutely not sustainable. We are coming to understand that we are going to have to change the way we live—radically change the way we live—not a tweaking here and there, not a light bulb change here or there, not a bicycle ride here or there—but a whole new way of seeing ourselves in relationship to other people and to the earth—living out of the consciousness of the sacredness of life.

And so today I would suggest we have a new frontier if we are to salvage this good earth and bequeath a future of any kind for coming generations. This new frontier is not "more," it's not "new and improved," as the ads go—it is not, in fact, what we will *have*, but what we will *become*. It is no longer an economic frontier, but a spiritual one.

Our President, Bill Sinkford, is about to speak to us on the subject "Choices That Matter." There has never been a time in the history of civilization when our choices mattered so much. Oh, there are many issues that all of us are passionate about—the war in Iraq, immigration reform with its overt racism, freeing ourselves of our oil addiction in this country, etc., etc. But all these issues converge at last into one—greed, empire building, short-term gain, long-term loss. The theological term for this is sin.

And so as a religious people, we have come together here at the edge of our country, to ask some questions: what does it mean to be a witness, in a time when the earth itself is endangered? What is our calling, as Unitarian Universalists, to help bring health and wholeness to this land? What does it mean to live with integrity in this brave new world we are about to enter?

We have too often been a people who have doubted our power. This is not the time for doubt, but the time for prayer, for re-grouping, for commitment, and for action. Welcome to the frontier.

WAY BEYOND TIME

PERSONAL ESSAY, UNPUBLISHED

2009

I have been a parish minister for seventeen years, and so I have watched a lot of people die. Being with people when they are dying is part of the job description. It may be the most important part, in fact. This is what I want to tell you about it: people are not afraid to die. Once they know, absolutely know and accept their dying, they are generally OK with it. They want to tell people they love good-bye. They want to know that they will not be forgotten. And they don't want to die alone. No one wants to die alone. I try to promise them that. Someone will be there.

Walt Whitman wrote in *Leaves of Grass*, "To die is different from what anyone supposed, and luckier." He should know. He was an ambulance driver during that slaughter that was the Civil War and was there with the dying a lot. The fear of death runs through our days, but when death comes, we make our peace with it.

I think about death a lot. I started in my mid-fifties. Both my parents were long dead by then, and gradually, one by one, the aunts and uncles died off: Aunt Ernie, Uncle Varnel, Aunt Bernadine, Uncle Lemos, Aunt Mellie, Uncle Gene, and finally last year, Aunt Sugar, an aunt by marriage. I'm among the next of the penguins to be pushed off the ice floe into the shark-invested waters, as a test for the others. They will watch and shake their penguin heads as I disappear below the surface, never to return. They will think to themselves, "Don't go there. Don't ever go there."

The problem is that we are animal creatures, and every cell in us tells us to choose life and avoid death. So even though I have witnessed many good deaths, I myself have not internalized my knowing. Sometimes death is called "the long sleep," and I comfort myself by thinking of it that way. But I know it isn't sleep, because one who sleeps will awaken to life once again, a facility unknown to the dead.

I keep remembering the little girl who came out of the hospital room after saying goodbye to her deceased grandmother and asked, "Is Grandma still dead?" No, death is not sleep. It is non-being, and I can't imagine non-being. Something about it just doesn't compute, and I get a lot of static when I turn on radio station DEAD.

I'm drawn frequently to the obituary page these days. I scan the dates: how many of these dead ones were born after I was, after 1941? And what did they die of? How are they remembered? Here are a few from today's obits in the *Oregonian*:

> Joy Louise (Williamson) Rahmig, born Aug. 11, 1949: "She was a personal banker."
>
> Kim Salem, born Oct. 1, 1959: "She was a 4-H secretary."
>
> Emma M. (Renke) Richardson, born June 9, 1912: "She was a homemaker."
>
> Harold Wolf, born May 15, 1921: "Harold was a violinist."

In most cases, we don't know the cause of death. We learn where the individual was born, what kind of work they did, who the survivors are, and where and when the funeral or memorial service is to be held. That's about it.

A few of the dead are pictured—these are the obituaries

paid for and written by family members. Unlike the journalist's objective summary, family writers use heartful adjectives and adverbs, words like "wonderful marriage" and "keenly interested in fashion" and "avid Oregon Ducks fan." A few add the family dog as one of the "survivors." Some will speak, rightly or wrongly, for the affections of the whole family and add a message such as "the family will miss him dearly."

This morning I am particularly drawn to the obituary of Charles Wesley Disbrow, III. He was born March 9, 1966, and died on January 21, 2010. That would make him only 44 when he died. He is pictured, and he is a perfectly gorgeous young man. And what an elegant name! Charlie (as he was apparently called) was a financial advisor who worked in Washington, D.C., and then Berkeley, California, before his work took him to Portland. He and his wife Katy had three sons, in whom he "encouraged athleticism," in particular his love of football. He was "keenly interested in others and had a cheerful, easygoing spirit that made him easy to be around." Charlie seems like such an all-American guy: good-looking, athletic, friendly, a family man. What illness or accident snatched him from us so soon? And why am I alive at 68 and Charlie dead at 44? Why?

I got married four months ago. When couples go to City Hall to get their marriage license in Portland, Oregon, they are directed to a computer to fill out a form. My husband-to-be, George, and I stood in line behind couples who seemed far too young to be getting married, and then it was our turn. Name, address, Social Security number. And then I noticed that the number 68 just popped up. "Why is 68 there?" I asked George.

"That's your age," he answered. "The computer got it from your Social Security information."

"That's not my age," I said, surprised. Surely this was a computer glitch. Surely I was 58. Maybe not 48, but surely not 68—58 sounded right.

George laughed. "Yes, it is. You are 68, and I am 72."

I felt dizzy, disoriented for a moment. I thought back to my last birthday party, just two months before. I remembered the heat of the July day, the smiles of my friends, the double chocolate birthday cake, the country music singer who performed "our song." I was 68. How did I get to be 68?

I remember a Gestalt workshop I attended, at a farm in Michigan, thirty years ago with a therapist named Neil Lamper. I was breaking free at the time—of marriage first, then of all lovers. And though I did not realize it at the time, I was breaking free of life as I had known it: my job, my home, my town, my friends, even my children.

I am in a circle of workshop participants, having chosen to "work" in the Gestalt way. I have on tight jeans and a close-fitting top, and I am aware of an energy moving in me, part sex, part anger, part sadness. I go around the circle and I look each person in the eye, and I say to each, in turn: "I am a 38-year-old woman." I am trying to believe my words. *How did I get to be 38?* I was 28 only yesterday. And so it goes.

I just got back from an aqua aerobics class. My first time there. I arrive early, and watch the others arrive. Older women, older than I am, I think, with lumpy thighs and fallen breasts. *I am not this old. I am in the wrong class.* The class turns out to be quite a workout though, and I have a little trouble with my balance.

The class is over, mercifully, in an hour. The young instructor smiles at me as I leave, and I smile back gingerly and thank her for the class. She tells me that balance becomes a problem "in older people," and then possibly seeing dismay written all over my face, she changes that statement to "that is, when people become older," and she goes on to warn, "they fall down and sometimes die just from the fall." She smiles. By the way, she says, I'm Marilyn. Me, too, I say. And I add, "I'm a swimmer, you know, and I'm taking the jazz dance class." *Just so she knows I'm not . . . infirm.* "I hope you come back," she says, and smiles again.

∞

Death somehow always comes as a surprise, as an aberration, though it is the experience that we surely hold most in common with all living things. We learn that we are "terminal," as they say of the place where you get off, the last stop, and we feel misjudged, even betrayed. *Won't I be the exception?*

Years ago one of my minister friends told me a story about a pastoral visit he had with a man who was 89 years old. The man had been told that he had cancer, and that the disease was advanced. He was "terminal." When my minister friend approached the man's hospital bed to bring him some comfort of whatever kind can come when there is nothing to be said, the old man looked at him, incredulous, and asked, "Why me?"

Five years later I am visiting that same minister friend. His name is Dan. Before he became a minister, he was a postman. Now he has brain cancer, and he is dying. The ministers of his acquaintance have pooled their money to buy him and his wife a new washing machine and dryer so they won't have to go across town to the laundromat. I was one of Dan's closest friends when we were seminary students, and I love the man, so I have flown down to say good-bye. His head is shaved from his surgeries, and he is thin. A Buddhist who has meditated for years, Dan is calm and quiet. On the other hand, I am frustrated and angry, and tears edge out in spite of myself. I want to rant and rave. Dan says, "It's all right. I'm all right." And I see that he is. He died a few weeks later. Every time I hear the band "Three Dog Night" I remember how Dan used to leap into the air as he danced to their music: "Joy to the world, all the boys and girls, joy to the fishes in the deep blue sea, joy to you and me."

∞

One of the most profound and important books in the English language, for my money, is Ernest Becker's *The Denial of Death.* Chapter 4 of this book, "Human Character as a Vital Lie," explains what he believes to be the core human problem. He begins the chapter by asking a question: "Why are so few people truly courageous?" The rest of the chapter unfolds with his answer.

To live courageously is to give up illusion. Giving up illusion is freeing of character and intent, but doing so forces us to face genuine despair. Our world is incomprehensible, "full of beauty, majesty, and terror," Becker writes. "Full humanness," he says, "means full fear and trembling, at least some of the waking day."

So any understanding that would make us feel weak or inferior or shameful—or of course *doomed*—must be repressed, to allow us to simply function. We imagine that we are in control of so much, and we are in control of so little. We can bear being alive only by lying to ourselves about ourselves and our world. And so because we escape from *knowing,* we fear death, but we also fear life. This is the process, psychologically necessary, by which we limit ourselves.

Most of us don't want to go there, thank you very much, and so we take another route. We make a cause or a country our reason for being. Or we fall in love. Or we make a whole shit-load of money. Or we become Number One, the Best, in whatever it is we do. Or we create something, some symbol of ourselves, that we think will never, never be destroyed (the transcendent Burj

Khalifa in Dubai). "Look on my works, ye mighty, and despair!" Anything at all to escape this fragile flesh. But we make our mark in shifting sand.

There is no earthly answer. None. Ernest Becker, the consummate scientist, the prodigious intellectual, having woven the threads of literature, theology, psychology, and psychiatry as few before him, finally arrives at this conclusion: "One must die and be reborn." Where have we heard this before? I hear Nicodemus asking Jesus, "How can a man be born when he is old? Can he enter the second time into his mother's womb, and be born?" It is the practical question of the materialist. *What can this possibly mean, to be born again?*

What it comes down to is this: we have to give up the pretense that we are secure, the easy confidence that has carried us through our days, oblivious. We find ourselves spiritually naked, hopelessly ignorant of the great mysteries of our lives. The ground we thought we were standing on is found to be mere invention. Furthermore, the nagging fear that we've kept at bay is now at the core, and taking over. And that's only the beginning. Like the newborn, we are all fear and longing. We know nothing.

Now we experience the "genuine despair" Becker speaks of. We've spent all the years of our life thus far developing our ego, making a "self" that can stand strong in the world, a unique person with a mission—only to find that there is no self at all, except the one that has been culturally created. It's a paper tiger. Ha-ha! The joke is on us.

It is then and only then when we are thrown back on an authentic faith, the faith that begins with renunciation of all certainty and exists in the service of Mystery, of What Is. Its hallmark is humility. As spiritual wisdom so often does, this choice rests in paradox: we give all that we have and all that we are to That Which We Absolutely Do Not Understand at All. This is your bare-bones faith—the only faith that's worth a nickel.

This faith is not constant, and there are times when it

comforts not at all. It most certainly does not banish anxiety, but merely makes it possible to trust that anxiety is a necessary part of the human condition, an unsettling that which reaches out for healing and wholeness.

∽

In Woody Allen's film *Manhattan*, Isaac, the protagonist, played of course by Allen himself, reasons in his desperate, flailing way, that if he is going to die anyway, why should he continue to live? It's a logical question. Life is hard. If we're going nowhere, if there's no destination, why make the difficult trip? Near the end of the film, Allen concludes that life itself is delicious enough, miraculous enough, to want to experience it, even if we know how the story will end. He sits alone in his apartment with a tape recorder and makes a list of things that give life meaning for him, including Groucho Marx, Marlon Brando, Louis Armstrong's "Potato Head Blues," those incredible apples and pears by Cezanne, the crabs at Sam Wo's. And of course, "Tracy's face."

Allen's protagonist comes to understand that he lives within the beauty and the majesty of this world, and he accepts the wonder of that as enough. He may not be heroic, as Becker would define it, but he is a practicing theologian. He descends, cascades, into thankfulness, the primal religious impulse. What's next? Maybe the crabs at Sam Wo's.

∽

It is true that once we accept, on a visceral level, that we are going to die one day, basic ontological questions appear. *So what's the deal?* Why am I enduring this pain (physical, emotional, psychological)? Why should I allow the ravages of old age to tear at me? Why, if

I'm going to lose everyone and everything, instead of anticipating it, shouldn't I just go ahead and do it now? Good-bye. Sayonara.

Some people have decided to not continue living. The philosopher and holocaust survivor Primo Levi was haunted by memories, and he died in a fall from a third-story landing, ruled a suicide. Carolyn Heilbrun, scholar and feminist writer, promised that she would kill herself when she got to be 70; she went on until she was 77 and then put a plastic bag over her head and did the deed. She was not sick, not mentally ill, not on medication. "That's the way she wanted it," her son is quoted as saying. Did she dread old age, with its accompanying failure of flesh and mind? Did she want to go out strong? And what is "strong" in this context, anyway?

When I was still a seminary student, I did a summer ministry at the Unitarian Universalist Fellowship in Boca Raton, Florida. There was a congregant named Herbert who came every Sunday to worship. He sat on the third row on my left, at the end. Every Sunday. He was 103 years old. One day Herbert asked me if I would come to visit him in his home, and so I did.

A minister never knows what will be needed, so after exchanging pleasantries and drinking tea, I waited for his question. "I don't know if my life is worth living," he said. "I can't give anything to anyone anymore."

I gulped. He's asking me THE BASIC QUESTION: why should I live? What could I say? So I said what was true for me. "Herbert, you are there in church every Sunday, there in your same seat. And every Sunday I come to preach, knowing that I will see you there. Do you know how much courage that gives me?"

He was quiet. I don't know if my answer was anything like adequate. He continued to attend church that summer, and I left for Berkeley to continue my studies. *He is part of that community, and when he is gone, there will be a hole in the sky. Doesn't he know?*

∞

I'm thinking of a woman of my acquaintance who took her own life. Though she was not an elderly woman, she had a difficult body to live with, one that caused her constant pain. She walked with a cane, grimacing and pulling herself along, step by step. As I remember, she had some financial problems and no real intimacy in her life. We visited one day, and she told me quite frankly that she was considering ending her life at some point. *Do you have a plan?* No. *Have you told others about this?* No. *Are you depressed?* No, I'm just tired of living, tired of struggling. I'm not saying I'm going to do it now. But it's a definite option, she told me.

Two months later she jumped off the Broadway Bridge into the cold, swirling waters of the Willamette River. No note. Her grown children knew what had happened, though, because she left a book with her glasses folded neatly upon it, on the bridge. As if she might come back and pick up where she left off. Her body wasn't found for weeks, and then it washed up on some far shore.

Sometimes you know when someone is going to die, because they start wrapping things up, saying good-bye. I should have known that's what Neil Lamper was doing when he showed up to see me installed as the Senior Minister of the First Unitarian Church in Portland, Oregon, eighteen years ago. He had been my Gestalt therapist at workshops he did at his farm in Allegan, Michigan; later he was my Gestalt teacher, and for a short while, my lover. A more alive person I have never known.

I didn't know Neil was among the eight hundred attendees, so many that we had to change the venue to First Methodist. It was a grand occasion, with me in my red doctoral robe trimmed in black velvet; there were welcomes by noted citizens, prayers, speeches, promises made, a sermon, music by the choir.

When all the drama was over, the benediction and recessional done, I went to the private room where I was to disrobe, and there he was, waiting for me, with that trickster grin that played upon his face when he was amused. I hadn't seen him in over a decade, but there he was. He didn't say a word at first, just held me close in his big arms.

When he released me, I saw in a glance the ravages of the cancer and the heart disease he had written me about: his face was lined, his hair whiter, and a front tooth was missing. *Why in God's name didn't he have that tooth repaired?*

After the reception, I insisted that he come home to stay with me for a few days. He had been sleeping at a cheap hotel on Burnside St., hanging out with the down-and-outs there for three days before the event. Not because he didn't have money. Just because that was his way.

Sex was out of the question, though neither one of us was partnered at that point. We were way beyond sex. He had continued to send me love letters full of erotic imagery for years after our sexual relationship was over. He continued, always, to tell me that he loved me. I knew that Neil loved many women. I was one of them. How special was I? I didn't know—until he turned up that night at the installation.

We talked about . . . well, what can I say? The meaning of life. Of our lives, our choices. Of what we didn't choose, as well as what we did. All the roads taken and not taken. He told me matter-of-factly about his cancer and his heart condition. He really didn't want to go into the details. He warned me not to let just any man have my heart. He could imagine, he said, that many men would see all that I had to offer—those long legs, yes, even the money I made—and would want me as their own. Wrong.

When he left, he made up his bed very carefully, perfectly, without a single wrinkle, and he gave me a gift, Jane Jacobs' *The Death and Life of Great American Cities.* He made a habit of never saying good-bye, so as he turned to leave, he grinned again and said, as I knew he would, "Catch you later."

During our visit he had told me about his friend Bonnie and her two-year-old and their plans to go to Australia. He had always wanted to live there, he said. And what a great kid, he loved that kid, he said. He didn't spend that much time with his own five kids when they were growing up, and now he just wanted to be with this kid, Bonnie's kid. And Bonnie, well, she was the most sexually uninhibited woman he had ever known.

Four or five months later, I guess it was, I got a call from Neil's daughter. I didn't know her at all. She said she found some letters, and she thought I would want to know. Neil was dead. He had moved to Australia, she said, with a woman named Bonnie and Bonnie's little girl, and two months later, he had a heart attack and died. He always wanted to move to Australia, she said, it was his dream. Yes, I said, yes, it was. And I thanked her for calling me.

That was eighteen years ago, eighteen years he has been gone. And yet he's still just as much alive in me as he ever was. Way beyond sex, way beyond time. *Catch you later.* So in what sense *is* he gone? In what sense is anyone ever really gone?

Just a few months ago, I picked up the Jacobs' volume and read it. The time has come round: the man I married is a city planner, and he's doing a book which takes off where her book ends.

Sages from various religious traditions have been telling us for centuries that we are irrevocably, immutably one. And now physicists have come to the same conclusion.

When the special theory of relativity blew apart a mechanistic universe, we found that time and space are not absolutes. And now quantum theory tells us there is no real distinction between a discrete object and its surroundings—in fact, we could say that *there is no such thing as a discrete object.* The universe has come to be regarded as an interconnected organism so elaborate that no portion of it can be clearly delineated from the whole of it.

At every moment, we choose and we create. We are not completely free, because the past informs the present, but every act is an unfolding, a connecting, and a cosmic surprise.

∞

John McPhee writes in the *New Yorker* (2/8/10) of his father's final days. The young attending physician is startlingly blunt in his message to the family. He says: "He can't comprehend anything, his eyes follow nothing, he is finished." At one point McPhee finds himself alone with his father, wondering what to do. Spontaneously he begins to talk, just "filling the air with words."

He tells his father, who had been a great fisherman, about his trip to New England, fishing in a canoe, casting. He goes into all the details: the inch of ice in the water bucket, his fingers turning red as he paddled, the ice actually freezing on the line. He goes on and on, blurting out everything he can remember about various species of fish. He calls up memories from fishing trips they had shared long ago.

He mentions that he had been fishing The Patch, his "home shore," where a big chain pickerel had been hiding. He had been using his father's bamboo rod, he says. He tells how, in that last cast before he had to go, the pickerel hit, taking the line down, wrapping it around the plants. "I pulled him out of there plants and all," McPhee says. "I caught him with your bamboo rod." He looks closely at his father, and he sees that his father's eyes have welled over.

∞

At the end pleasure will go. The love of good food will go. Dignity won't matter any more. Even prayers will fall away. The last thing a dying person is conscious of is the human voice. Connection is all that is left. We learn that it is all that ever really mattered.

What will we leave behind? Every little thing that we have given. Every little place we have touched in. We have perhaps plaited hair. Designed a building. Written a poem. Placed bricks to make a wall. Held a screaming infant. Made a pudding. Saved a stream. Played a violin. Planted a tree. Taken a picture. Written a letter. Buried a pet. Listened to a friend. Just showed up.

It all remains, way beyond time. *Catch you later.*

THE USES OF POWER

ESSAY IN *THE GROWING CHURCH: KEYS TO CONGREGATIONAL VITALITY*

ED. THOM BELOTE

2010

In order to counter British imperialism, some native citizens of Northern Rhodesia were using Gandhi and his teaching of non-violent resistance as their guide. They simply refused to co-operate with the colonial government. The British colonists, on the other hand, were wary of living in a country where their presence was not supported.

After putting up with this resistance for several months, the British government sent a new, particularly tough administrator to the colony, a disciplined man who would surely bring these recalcitrant Africans in line, they thought. However, when the new administrator arrived at the Lusaka airport, he had a surprise waiting for him. Julia Chikamonenga had organized a group of women, the biggest women she could find, to welcome their new ruler. As he got off the plane, he saw before him a vast sea of naked Zambian women, singing songs of greeting. He turned tail, got back on the plane, and ordered the pilot to fly, post haste, back to London.*

* This story is recounted by Vern Huffman in "Stories from the Cha Cha Cha," pp. 161-2 of *The Impossible Will Take a Little While*, ed., by Paul Rogat Loeb, New York: Basic Books, 2004.

This is a story about power. It is a story about the misuse of power, in that colonialism never has moral grounding; rather, it is exploitation based on military and economic superiority. But the story is about another kind of power—the power of people who just said no, who would not co-operate with their oppressors. And it is about native ingenuity and humor—informal power of the people—that turned the tables on the formal power of the colonizing country. These women, who seemed to have so little worldly power, pulled a kind of aikido move on the British.

Power is exercised by all human beings. We soon learn to leverage our gifts to gain advantage of one kind or another. And there are all kinds of power. Some people have great intellectual power, others charisma, others good looks, and still others wealth or charm or talent. Some hold high office, some are physically strong, others have family ties or reputation. Still others can draw sympathy or attention by their very neediness. In and of itself, power is neither good nor evil: it is morally neutral. It can be used for nefarious ends, or it can be used to heal and to bring justice. It just depends on the spiritual maturity of the one who wields the power, and the purpose for which it is used.

So if power per se is not evil, why is there so much fear of power? We fear power in others, and many of us fear power in ourselves. Perhaps we believe Lord Acton's dictum "Power corrupts, and absolute power corrupts absolutely." And it is true that where there is great power, there is great temptation to disregard or to misuse those subject to one's power. There is ample justification for our fears, given the terrible misuses of power that we have seen in various arenas, only recently. We have seen an administration in Washington that for eight years has abused power in starting an illegal war, condoning torture, constraining civil rights. We have seen the Catholic Church shamed because of priests who used the power of their office to molest children, while the administration of the Church looked the other way.

We have seen business people allow their greed and carelessness to bring about untold economic hardship for millions of citizens.

So, yes, we have reason to be fearful. We may have seen ourselves misuse power as we discipline our children or as we speak in a certain tone to our employees. And we are wary of those who have power of any kind over us, rightfully doubtful that those parties will use their power well. Yet when our distrust of power makes us reluctant to become powerful and to exercise our power, much is lost to the world.

Let us examine the term more closely. Power is not the acting, so much as it is the potential or the possibility of acting. The word *power* comes from the Latin *potere*, meaning "to be able." If one is powerful, then, one is able, one is potent, one is capable. When we look at the Indo-European roots of the word, however, we find that the root of the word power is *poti*, meaning master or lord; from the Greek, *posis* means husband. And so the element of dominance or control begins to rear its ugly head.

It is the feminists who have most consistently questioned the idea of dominance in relationships, most notably Riane Eisler, who speaks of the "partnership society" as opposed to the "dominance model" of the patriarchy. So the question arises: can we act, can we exercise power—or indeed can we *dominate*—without domination becoming onerous? An adjunct question is whether or not we should do away with hierarchy in our organizational life.*

I am a feminist. I want women to be unafraid of their power and to contribute more fully to political, academic, clerical, and business life of our nation. I am also a mother and have served as the senior minister of a large church, and both of those experiences have taught me that exercising power through dominance and control is not only acceptable, but essential in order to accomplish certain ends—parental in the case of the one, and organizational,

* James Hillman asks these important questions in his book *Kinds of Power: a Guide to Its Intelligent Uses*, New York: Doubleday, 1995, pp. 98-99.

in the case of the other. Furthermore, I believe that hierarchy is the only workable way to structure large organizations.

Let's define some terms, before we go further. Definition is important, because it is generally the connotation of certain words rather than the denotation that concerns us. By *dominance,* I mean "to exert the determining or guiding influence." Further, *dominate* means "to have, or to exert mastery." This is what leaders do. They do not, as one lay leader explained it to me, "put a leash on the big dog, and then follow where that dog pulls you." The "dog" might pull you, for example, to capital punishment. Or in earlier days, into a lynch mob. Leaders have vision, and they often go against the grain. In fact, by definition, they must be self-differentiated and they must see beyond what *is* to what could and must be.

So what about control? To say that someone has "a controlling personality" is not a compliment. And yet we all admire those people who can take control when the situation calls for it. We talk about "crowd control," the absence of which brings chaos and even death. We all are familiar with the situation in which the facilitator of a question/answer session is passive and allows audience members to drone on with lengthy comments of their own, ignoring the needs of the group. *Why doesn't the leader take control?* we think. Presumably, we want a President of the United States who has a strong sense of control, given all the forces coming at him. This does not mean that our President will ignore the views of others, will fail to be respectful, will be unwilling to learn and change his mind. But he best be in control of his staff, else his staff will be in control of him. *Control* by definition simply means "the power or authority to manage."

I am advocating for leadership here. And I am speaking for leadership grounded in a formal structure, so that everyone in the organization knows who is responsible for what, and who is accountable to whom. I have seen feminist friends try to "level" everyone in an organization—that is, make everybody equal in decision-making. In two cases, these were law firms run by feminists. In one of these, everyone had a say, and everyone was paid the same amount, including the secretaries and file clerks. The firm soon dissolved into chaos; moreover, the professionals could not bring in enough money to make payroll. The second law firm was started by three female friends, all of whom were to have an equal voice. Within a year, the firm had broken up, and the most capable, most dominant lawyer started her own firm. The third example was a non-profit: three feminists convinced the Board that they would run the organization as co-directors. Within a year, all three were looking for new jobs. I have seen one too many ministers calling themselves "co-ministers" when they were not equal either in power or in salary, making the title misleading and confusing, ultimately causing conflict and sometimes untimely resignations.

When organizational structure is formal and clear, communication flows easily, questions are answered readily, and responsibility is taken. On the other hand, when leadership of an organization is ambiguous, the result is confusion about responsibilities and bottle-necking around decision-making. There is no such thing as a "leaderless group," for if there is no assigned or elected leader, an informal leader will emerge. When power structures are unclear, power will be exercised in covert ways, under the table, instead of exercised openly by persons who are accountable for decisions.

In terms of power structures, then, we should distinguish between those schemes that make for clarity, efficiency, and responsibility, thereby serving the mission of the organization, and those that exist to repress the contributions and creativity of the many because of the fears or unhealthy ego needs of the leader.

Those who actively seek power because they are fearful and insecure are the least able to handle it well, whereas spiritually mature leaders are eager not only to move the mission of the organization forward, but also to give every opportunity for all individuals on the team to flourish and to develop to their fullest potential. It should be said that to exercise power at all requires self-confidence, or ego strength. The only question is whether the individual is acting chiefly from ego needs, or is in service to something larger than himself. Power that is colored by ambition, tyranny, selfishness, and greed is to be noted and resisted. Power used in the service of others should be honored and upheld.

TRAVELING BY YOUR OWN LIGHTS

KEYNOTE ADDRESS AT BRIGHT LIGHTS AWARDS BANQUET
PORTLAND, OREGON
2010

Good evening! These stories this evening have just been amazing, haven't they, and humbling. If you're like me, you're moved and inspired—and maybe you're thinking, wow, I couldn't do something like that: I couldn't start a non-profit from scratch, like Katy Kolker with her Fruit Tree Project, and harvest 15,000 pounds of fruit the first year—or like Dick and Jeanne Roy, with their ecology institute that reaches all over the country. And on and on. Everyone honored tonight is a kind of hero.

But after all, these are all ordinary people, just like you and me—ordinary people who have done extraordinary things. We didn't have time to hear the genesis of their ideas, to hear about the fears they may have had, to hear about the struggles—you know, the things that went wrong before they knew how to set things right. Still, hearing these stories gives us pause, perhaps—makes of think of our own lives and the trajectory our own lives are on.

When I reached my 50's, I started following the obituaries in the newspaper—you folks middle-aged and older will relate to this: you begin to understand that you have a limited amount of time left on this earth, and you want to make the most of it. Anyway, I started collecting obituaries of people I admired and putting their pictures up on my fridge—in fact, I had a sermon entitled "Dead People on My Fridge." (Not *in* my fridge, you understand, *on* my fridge!) I put Richard Avedon, the photographer up there; I put Mr. Rogers; there's Johnny Cash, Lynn Redgrave, and Daniel Schorr.

Now what do all these people have in common? They're not fabulously good-looking, any one of them—well, maybe Johnny Cash is. Yes, each one has talent, has gifts—but so does everyone have gifts. The thing that they have in common is that they each had a vision that was their own, and they followed it. No matter what other people said, no matter what had been done in the past. No matter what they had to give up, to become their very own selves, not a copy of anyone else, but their very own unique selves. They all had that strange and elusive quality that we call "integrity."

Sometimes in our personal journey a possibility rises up before us, and it is possibility that frightens us the most. Here is a book I could write! (And the voice comes whispering, "Who do you think you are, to write a book?") Or a path opens before us, and fear grabs us by the throat.

I'm thinking of a young man who came into my office one day to talk about his calling. He said to me, "I think I'm supposed to go to seminary, but I'm afraid."

"And why are you afraid?" I asked.

"I come from a poor background," he said.

I just looked at this beautiful, bright, gentle young man, and I said, "So you're afraid? So? I'm afraid, too. Everybody's afraid. We can't let that stand in the way of our calling." (I belong to the "kick-ass" school of ministry.)

So we fear we might mess up, flame out. Or we feel that we might not be accepted. I know of a person who dreads the end of his Shabbat service because the rabbi always says to turn to the person next to you and say, "Shabbat Shalom." This individual has the terrible fear that the person next to him won't want to reciprocate—that he'll put out his hand, and the other person won't respond. It has never happened. It's an irrational thought, of course. But this kind of thing strikes at something deep within, some subconscious learning that has wormed its way into our flesh. We'll reach out to someone, and we'll be rejected. We'll set out on a challenging project, and we'll screw it up, and everybody will know. How often do our irrational fears keep us from our deepest longings? What would you choose to do if you knew beyond a doubt that you would succeed?

Sometimes, I regret to say, I've tried to be less than I am—for women, in particular for women of my generation—that's an ever-present temptation. Women are supposed to be quiet nurturers, not bold leaders. And I'm here to tell you—both men and women—agreeing to shrink down, to be "less than," is a dead end proposition. The reasons for agreeing to be smaller than you are, are myriad. You can pull back because of your social class, like this young man—if you grew up poor or working class, you may never have been taught that you don't have the same rights and privileges as others. You can pull back because you've been abused and misused and neglected, and you've learned, incorrectly, that you're somehow at fault for everything that's wrong in the family. You can pull back because you're a gay man or a lesbian woman, and some people, even in progressive Portland, want to put you down. You may hear your father's voice telling you to "succeed" on his terms, not your own. There may be your mother's voice, telling you to live her unlived life.

The people we admire the most travel by their own lights. At the same time, they are not ego-driven. They know that their lives do not belong to themselves alone, but belong to life itself. Their lives are given over to something larger than themselves.

To claim your own strength and beauty, your own goodness and creativity, requires courage. There will be practical hindrances, always—there'll be this, there'll be that—there'll be excuses to be made—and of course there will always be fears.

The Quaker educator Parker Palmer tells a personal story that helps us know what to do when we get to those tough places that we can't seem to get through.*

* Parker Palmer, *Let Your Life Speak: Listening for the Voice Within*, Jossey-Bass, 2000, pp. 82-85.

He says that in his early '40's he decided to go on an Outward Bound program. He was kind of depressed, and he thought that the challenge of the program might wake him up, teach him a few things. He chose a week-long course at Hurricane Island—the name itself, he says, should have warned him. It was not called Pleasant Valley.

Anyway, around the middle of the week, he found himself facing the challenge he feared the most. One of the instructors led him up to the edge of a cliff 110 feet above the ground, tied a thin rope to his waist, and told him to start "rappelling" down the cliff. "Just go!" the instructor said.

So Parker went, and immediately crashed into a rocky ledge. The instructor said, "I don't think you've quite got it."

"Right," said Parker, "So what am I supposed to do?"

"The only way to do this," the instructor said, "is to lean back as far as you can—you have to get your body at right angles to the cliff. It's counterintuitive, but it's the only way that works."

Parker thought he had to be wrong, of course. Obviously, he should hug the mountain, staying as close to the rock as possible. Once again he tried, and once again slammed with force into the next ledge. So then Parker decided to risk it all: "he leaned back into empty space, his eyes fixed on the heavens in prayer, and started descending the rock face." It worked! He became more and more confident with each step.

When he was about halfway down, another instructor called up from below: "Parker, I think you'd better stop and see what's just below your feet." Parker slowly lowered his eyes and saw beneath him a great gaping hole in the side of the rock wall. He knew he would have to change direction, and he was quite sure when he did, he would die. He froze.

The second instructor allowed him to hang there, shaking with fear, for what seemed like forever. Finally she shouted her helpful advice: "Parker, is anything wrong?"

Parker says he still cannot imagine where his words came

from, but several people later say that he said, in childlike voice, "I don't want to talk about it."

"Then," said the second instructor, "It's time you learned the Outward Bound motto."

"Great," Parker thought. "I'm about to die, and she's going to give me a motto."

Then the instructor yelled out ten words he says he never wants to forget. The rest of his days he has felt their weight and meaning of what he heard: "If you can't get out of it, get into it!" He writes that these words bypassed his brain, went into his body, and gave movement to his legs. His feet seemed to move of their own accord, and shortly he made it to the ground safely.

"If you can't get out of it, get into it." You know, the fact is, that most people who do great things in this world are not geniuses—and as I said they are often not more gifted than many others. The difference is that these people have the courage to live the life they were called to live: it's that they are never afraid—it's that they don't run from their fear: they invite it in, get into it, own it, and it loses its power over them. As you meet resistance, you will discover strength, beauty, depth, you never knew you had.

The question is not, how can I "be successful," how can I find the perfect life, but how do I live the life that is mine, the one "wild and precious life," as Mary Oliver says, the one wild and precious life that I have been given. This is your life, yours and no other's. Live it freely, giving your talents, your love, your knowing, as no one else can. Seek out those people who celebrate what you are; seek out those places where you are encouraged to become every inch of what you were meant to become. And in so blessing the world, you will find that you are greatly blessed.

THE THEOLOGY OF UNITARIAN UNIVERSALISTS

HUFFINGTON POST

2010

How many times have I heard people remark, "You can believe anything and be a Unitarian Universalist." Or someone might say, with no trace of irony, "I go to the Unitarian Universalist church because I don't believe in organized religion." Incredulous, I say to myself, "Gee, I try to be organized. And we do have a choir. And choir robes. And ministers. And a building."

Unitarian Universalism is a religion—and one with a long and noble history. Why are we so often misunderstood? One problem is our public relations gaffes. All too often when Unitarian Universalists have gotten in the national news, it has been because of some P.R. blunder, like the minister who, during the worst of the AIDS epidemic, passed out free condoms during the Sunday service and spoke on the subject, "The Condom Conundrum." This was not a bad idea—it's just not what most churches in the nation were doing on Sunday morning. Or the student minister (she never actually made it into our ministry) who had a funeral service, with communion, for her dog and invited all of the cats and dogs in her Berkeley neighborhood to the service. The AP wire photo showed a dog standing on its hind legs, its mouth open for the communion wafer, and the article stated, "The guests neither barked nor balked at receiving the host."

We are a free religious faith, and so have no creed. And as freedom is wont to do, our faith invites a certain degree of wackiness and abuse. But if that's the price of freedom, then I still choose freedom.

Our faith, of course, does have requirements. To become a Unitarian Universalist, you make no doctrinal promises, but you are required to do much more. You are required to choose your own beliefs—you promise, that is, to use your reason and your experience and the dictates of your conscience to decide upon your own theology, and then you are asked to actually live by that theology. You are asked to take your chosen faith very seriously.

In a very real sense, all theology is autobiography, is it not? Our experience, real and vicarious, is what informs our sense of reality, our internal picture of the way the world works, what our values are. We believe what we know is true—that is, our felt knowledge—not what we are told is true. In the final analysis, how can a person who wishes to live with integrity do other than this?

Our free faith was hard won. It has a long history, and our religious ancestors died for this freedom.

A Unitarian, King John Sigismund of Transylvania—now known as Romania—pronounced the first edict of religious freedom in the year 1568. I traveled to Romania several years ago and stood in the church in Torda, where that proclamation was made. This was an almost unimaginable act in an age in which people were being burned at the stake for not getting their theology just right.

Francis David, King Sigismund's spiritual advisor, was the single greatest influence on the king's theological beliefs. After Sigismund's death, David lost favor and was finally arrested for his views. I made a pilgrimage to the town of Deva and walked up a long, dusty hill to the dungeon where he was imprisoned. It was actually a deep hole in the ground into which David was lowered, and there he sickened, and died. His famous words still live with us, though. He said simply, "You need not think alike to love alike." At the center of our faith is not belief, but love.

Many others died for their faith during this period of religious persecution. The Unitarian movement came out of the left wing of the Protestant Reformation, and we were way too far to the left for both Calvin and Luther. The Unitarian scholar Servetus, who wrote *On the Errors of the Trinity*, was burned in effigy by the Catholics and then burned in fact by Calvin, with a copy of his book strapped to his thigh. It is said that if he had been willing to change just one word of his book—to change "Jesus is a son of God" to "Jesus is the son of God"—he could have saved his life.

So this is our heritage—or at least a little taste of it. It is rich, and we can be proud of it. This is not light or easy stuff that we're a part of. But because we are a free faith, could our movement be said to have a theology? After all, our contemporary churches are populated with Christians, atheists, humanists of various stripes, Jews, Buddhists, and even Wiccans. Whoever will, may come. Nevertheless, when we look at our history and the practice of our faith, certain theological themes dominate, and so I will argue that, yes, we do have in fact a theology of sorts, a theology that has been relatively clear and consistent through time.

We must begin with the assertion that Unitarian Universalism has always emphasized freedom as a core value. It follows that human beings have a choice. We are not predestined by God before our births, to be saved or unsaved. We are not mired in original sin by the very fact of our birth and therefore have to go through a ceremony called baptism, even as babies, to cleanse ourselves of that sin. We do not have to have someone sacrifice himself by dying on a cross to save us from hell. Yes, human beings have a propensity to do evil, but we also have the propensity to do great good. We have a choice. Unitarian Universalists prefer to think of ourselves as being born into "original blessing," as theologian Matthew Fox likes to put it. (He was of course ex-communicated from the Catholic Church, for that heresy and others.)

The term "Unitarian" indicates our belief that God is One. As Church doctrine began to be codified in the fourth century, the concept of the trinity was found to be confusing for our Catholic forebears, and they disagreed with their colleagues in the church hierarchy. But when the vote was taken in 325, the Nicene Creed was adopted, and the doctrine of the trinity was established. Note that the trinity is not a Biblical concept—it originated in the power structure of the Catholic Church. Basically, the Unitarians lost the vote.

The concept that God is One goes beyond the controversy over the trinity, however. If God is One, then the God of the Jews and the God of the Muslims and the God of the Christians is One. God is One. I remember a tragic incident that occurred during my ministry. One evening I was called to the hospital to be with the mother of a two-year-old child who was brain-dead after choking on a piece of chewing gum. The mother, a Unitarian Universalist, was estranged from the child's father, who was of another faith. Leaving the hospital, I found myself in the elevator with the father's minister, and I said to him, "Well, we can do the memorial service together." And he responded, "No, we can't. We don't worship the same God." His comment made my sadness deeper still, and the estrangement of these families seemed ever greater. What other God could he have been thinking of?

As Unitarian Universalists, we respect other religious traditions—we don't think we have the market on the truth. I like the way my late colleague, Dr. Forrest Church of All Souls in New York, put it. He said that truth is like light shining through the windows of a great cathedral, in different colors and shapes. The light comes from the same source. But it looks different, depending upon which window it shines through. So it is with the various religious traditions of our world. In conducting worship, I regularly use readings from a wide range of sources, including Native American, ancient Chinese, the Hebrew Bible, Rumi, as well as a lot of contemporary poetry. Truth is where you find it. There is no single scripture that holds all the truth.

And there's another theological perspective that Unitarian Universalists have concerning truth: we believe in evolution—not only evolution of life forms, but evolution of thought and evolution of moral and ethical understanding. So the truth that I embrace today may not be the truth I embrace tomorrow. Revelation is not static, but is ever unfolding. More and more will be revealed. Our part is simply to be open, and thirsty, thirsty for the truth that would be ours—but just for the time being. Such a stance keeps us humble—and awake. When we venture into the Mystery, we are entering the ground of the infinite with the powers of a finite mind. An awe-filled agnosticism is perhaps the better part of wisdom.

Unitarian Universalist theology is of this world, not of the next. Jesus, in fact, taught that the Realm of God is within and, contrary to most Christian practice, his teachings were centered on relationship, not salvation. Unitarian Universalists do not emphasize an afterlife. For one reason, we simply don't know anything about it. No one as yet has come back to report. But we do know about suffering and injustice on this earth, and so we try to create the Kingdom of Heaven here and now, with real people.

Back to Francis David—our faith is focused not on what we believe, but how we love. It is a fact that people with the most fervent and orthodox beliefs have been known to engage in some of the most dastardly acts. Christopher Hitchens and other prominent non-believers take great pleasure in pointing out this discrepancy in religious faith. I would agree with Hitchens that the rise of fundamentalism in various parts of our world is one of the most frightening of contemporary social and political developments. When we place another beneath us, set apart from us, we tear out a part of our human heart, and then anything goes, for that person has become Other. For Unitarian Universalists, the question is never "What do you believe?" but rather "What kind of person have you become? What are the fruits of your living?"

The significance of love and tolerance in our faith is even more strongly a dimension of Universalism. The Universalist movement began in our country in the late 18th century, about the same time as did the Unitarian movement, both being imports from England. The American Universalist preacher Hosea Ballou told his followers that heaven and hell are not found in any kind of afterlife, but simply in the life we create on this earth. He also rejected the idea that Jesus's death on the cross saved us—he taught that what saved us was Jesus's embodiment of love and justice. Historically, paradise for the Universalist was a place where people struggle with injustice and where they are called upon to develop wisdom and our capacity to love.

The universalism in Universalist refers to universal salvation, a very radical theological concept that emerged in an age in which revival preachers were riding through the countryside telling people that they were going to burn in hell unless they repented of their sins. I remember the time I was speaking at a conference on Buddhist-Christian dialogue, and at lunch one of the Christian presenters, a noted academic, said to me, "This doctrine of Universalism, that's a pretty silly notion, don't you think?" I was taken aback, and I said no, that actually I thought it was a step in the right direction at a time when hell and damnation sermons were giving God a bad name. And then I paused, and I said to him, "Do you believe that God loves everyone?"

"Yes," he said.

"So did God love Hitler, too?"

Reluctantly, he agreed. "Yes, I suppose so," he said.

And then I said, "And so it's not that much of a stretch, is it, to believe that a loving God could somehow in the end, reconcile all things to Himself." And we let the conversation end there.

The Unitarians and Universalists talked for many years about merging, and although their theologies were close, they were kept apart by class differences. The Unitarians tended to come from the educated, upper-middle class, and tended to be more cerebral in their worship style than the Universalists, who were mainly rural and less well educated. They decided in 1961, at last, to merge and now the faith is known as Unitarian Universalist.

In summary, we Unitarian Universalists do have a theology:

- We believe that human beings should be free to choose their beliefs according to the dictates of their own conscience.
- We believe in original goodness, with the understanding that sin is sometimes chosen, often because of pain or ignorance.
- We believe that God is One.
- We believe that revelation is ever unfolding.
- We believe that the Kingdom of God is to be created here on this earth.
- We believe that Jesus was a prophet of God, and that other prophets from God have risen in other faith traditions.
- We believe that love is more important than doctrine.
- We believe that God's mercy will reconcile all unto itself in the end.

Now this piece about God's mercy—I confess that I don't know how that could be true. How could God's love be that encompassing, that forgiving? I can't even forgive my neighbor who consistently gets out his leaf blower while I'm trying to write a sermon. How could everyone be saved? Surely some of us should go to hell! Surely the guy with the leaf blower.

No, not one. Not one, in God's infinite mercy. And we are asked to stretch ourselves large enough to take that in. I'm not there yet. But that's the great thing about my faith. It's evolving. And so am I. May God have mercy upon my soul. And yours. So be it. Amen.

THE DEATH OF OSAMA BIN LADEN

BLOG, MARILYN SEWELL

2011

I find myself deeply disturbed by the death and collective responses to the death of Osama bin Laden. When I say "disturbed," I don't mean merely intellectually, but psychologically, spiritually, and even physically. I have found myself drained of energy, withdrawn. And I've had to ask myself why. Shouldn't I be happy, gratified that a monster of evil is now gone from the face of the earth? I note the celebrating crowds on television, in New York and Washington, D.C., and understand their very human response, but I'm not there.

I think my disturbance comes from having to contend with conflicting values that all have their measure of truth—and yet none has the whole truth. And so I'm trying to reconcile these disparate values.

With the rest of the nation, I have witnessed the overwhelming grief of the families of the 9/11 victims. I have seen the pictures of the dead, read their stories. I have heard the goodbye messages of spouses, the children left without a father, the way victims jumped to their deaths, some holding the hand of a friend. I understand why the survivors want justice, and whatever closure they can find, and so they welcome the news of bin Laden's death.

I also understand the significance for our nation, in bin Laden's death. He has been not only the perpetrator of much suffering and death, but he had become the symbol of our impotence in failing to rid the world of terrorism. He has been thumbing his nose at us for ten years, making us fear what might happen next. The President's main job is to protect his people, and so Obama had to pursue Osama bin Laden and kill him.

Which brings me to the next point. I have little doubt that the Seals were ordered to kill Bin Laden, whether or not he was armed, whether or not he surrendered. Taking bin Laden prisoner would have invited an international media circus for a trial that might have lasted years—and further provoked all kinds of national and international conflict. We weren't going to let that happen. He was going to be killed and then buried at sea. He was shot first in the chest, I would guess, as would be the normative first shot, and then shot in the head, to assure the death. I also understand the necessity of this decision, and if in fact I am correct, I do not fault Obama for proceeding in this way.

On the other hand, I am a minister and a wife and a mother. I abhor violence. In particular, gun violence disturbs me, for I have personally lost family members to gun violence, as have so many others in our gun-crazy country.

And then I imagine the scene in the compound that night. I imagine the fear that everyone in that compound must have felt as the Seals attacked. I expect Osama bin Laden knew he was going to die. One of his wives watched him shot to death, another identified the body. A number of his children were present in compound. What did the wives and children experience?

Still another dimension to this whole scene is that of the warriors. The Seals carried out what appears to have been an almost flawless plan in dangerous circumstances: their courage and skill are admired by all. And yet the man who killed bin Laden and whoever killed the three others will have to live with the memory of that night: the fear in the eyes of those who were killed or wounded, the gaping wounds, the blood pouring out—all this, and the knowledge that they took a human life. This is what we ask of our warriors. To do these horrific deeds for us. We don't want to see the pictures. Obama spared us from that.

So what it comes down to, for me, is this: the terrible grayness of morality. The evil that we're all drawn into. The violence that is a part of our lives. The fallenness of us all. There are no good guys and bad guys, except in relative terms. We can only try to see as clearly as we can and act with as much integrity as we can. The Kingdom of God is not as yet at hand. Heaven help us.

FORGIVENESS AND THE LAW OF LOVE

HUFFINGTON POST

2011

It is an unfortunate truth that happiness and good fortune rarely deepen us spiritually. It is when we run into unbearable grief and loss we are unprepared for that we are stripped of our vanity and our pride and begin to see, rock-bottom, what is really important to us. These occasions are what I call "leveling experiences" because they let us know that we, along with all human beings, are mortal and vulnerable. At these times so much of our anger and hard-heartedness seems petty, for we come to understand that all human beings suffer immeasurably as they journey through life, and we join them as fellow sufferers on the path. We gain a measure of humility, we become more compassionate and more forgiving.

Profound spiritual lessons can come from those who provoke us the most. People we can hardly bear to be around, the ones who "hook" us emotionally, are the ones who carry our unconscious stuff around, bringing it uncomfortably close to the surface. We want to run, not walk, in the other direction. But we find we are looking in a mirror of sorts. We are led to ask ourselves, "What part of my shadow is this person asking me to uncover and examine?" These individuals are the ones who can stretch us the most, spiritually speaking.

We also grow in our ability to forgive as we reflect upon the circumstances of our own lives. We realize that even our best-intentioned, most spirit-led decisions have the capacity to hurt others, including those we love. We have made mistakes, misjudgments, careless errors, perhaps, that have led to pain for others or even tragic consequences. In fact, there is no way for even the best intentioned, most moral individual to go through a life without hurting others. So each of us has to live with the consequences of our own inevitable harming of others, even when we would do only good—never mind when we have been motivated by less than noble motives. This understanding helps us forgive those who have, for whatever reason, known or unknown, caused us to suffer. We, too, have caused others to suffer. "All have sinned and come short of the glory of God," as my saintly grandmother used to remind me regularly.

My father has been dead for almost 20 years now, but I remember having a conversation with him when I was a young adult. It was an awkward conversation. We somehow got around to talking about my growing-up days, and my father asked at one point, "I was a pretty good dad, wasn't I? I gave you whatever you needed didn't I?" My memory was different from that. I remembered that money was scarce, that my father threw it away on alcohol and gambling.

"Well, actually, no, you didn't . . . you weren't . . . actually, our childhood was pretty difficult, Daddy." My father's face hardened in pain, and he said, "When you get older, you'll see. You'll see, when you have children of your own." And he was right. Yes, he hurt me grievously through his drinking, the same drinking that came between him and my mother, but I came to see that his alcoholism was not about me. It was about his emotional suffering from way back in his childhood and about his losing our mother, the only woman he ever loved, and about the addictive disease that alcohol is.

Another person's behavior is really not about us. Most of the time, the harm another does comes out of ignorance, pain, neediness and confusion—the very same qualities that push us to act in ways we really don't want to act.

I did, in fact, find out what he meant by "I would see, when I had children of my own." He hurt his children, though he loved us. And though I loved them, I hurt my own children when I divorced their father. I can rationalize and say that they would have been worse off had I stayed with him, but I don't know that that's true. I know that I would have been worse off, and I was not willing to live half a life, with possibilities cut off. Will my children forgive me? I hope they will. We all cause pain, and we all need forgiveness.

We need to be careful of piety—that is, the dutiful obedience that is so often tinged with self-righteousness and pride. One of the most fascinating stories in the Hebrew Bible is the story of the Prodigal Son. You may remember the story: a wealthy landowner has two sons, the older one, who follows his father's every wish, and the younger one, who is something of a hell-raiser. So the younger son tells his father, "Give me my inheritance." (Read: "I don't want to wait until you kick off. I want to party on, now!)

So the father does as his son asks. The son goes into a far land and spends all his inheritance in profligate living, and when he runs out of money, he runs out of friends. He finds himself caring for the animals on a pig farm, and he realizes, "Why, even these pigs have better food than I have! I should go back home and tell my father that I really screwed up, and that I'm sorry." And that he does.

When his father sees him coming in the distance, he says to his servants, "Kill the fatted calf! Invite my son's friends over for a party!" The son approaches his father, falls to the ground and begs for forgiveness, and the father puts a ring on his finger and rejoices, for that which was lost has been found.

Now, the really interesting part to the story to me is the reaction of the older brother. He says to his father, "Father, you never killed a calf for me, never even killed a goat, for me and my friends. So how come he disobeyed you, left home, wasted all your money and now he gets all the goodies? I've obeyed you all these years, and I get nothing."

Which brother would you like to have for a friend? Which one would you like to go out for an evening with? Sometimes we have to make mistakes—and big ones—before we learn a better way. But we are apt to grow richer and deeper, as we experience the bumps and bruises. Sometimes we bump and bruise others, as well. But how much more desirable this path, than the way of this prig of an older brother, who holds himself back from life and experience, and who judges himself worthy and his younger brother unworthy. Why could he not be happy at his brother's return? His piety had stolen his joy, his ability to rejoice in his brother's redemption. He is the big loser in the story.

The problem with piety—and self-righteousness, in general—is that it separates us from others. In the safe and secure citadel of our own goodness, we place ourselves out of human reach. The law is what directs us, then, and mercy takes a back seat. We become blind to our own failings, so intent are we on judging others, and in fact on projecting our own flaws onto them. A person can follow all the rules and yet be lacking in the milk of human kindness. In fact, when people are too rule-driven, that is what generally results.

The one law that is large enough to contain all the lesser laws, the one law that must be considered the grounding of the life well lived, is the law of love. If that law is grossly violated, it really doesn't matter how much money we make or how many accolades we receive. If we are able to live by this larger law, we will find within ourselves a kind and understanding heart, both for ourselves and for others. Forgiveness will come more easily because we know how morally frail we ourselves are, because we ourselves have blundered and because we know that the story is not over, that redemption is possible.

It is comforting to me to remember that my very weaknesses

form the tension that pulls me again and again to the Holy One, asking that my brokenness be made whole. Paradoxically, it is often when I feel most satisfied with myself that I find myself losing faith—or becoming, as it were, faithless. Self-congratulatory, I say to myself, "I'm doing great . . . wasn't I?" Humility makes space for the Holy in our lives, whereas self-righteousness and judgment alienate others and elbow God out, as well.

It seems to me that forgiveness is all of a piece: when we are unable to forgive, we then perpetuate the fruits of non-forgiveness—anger, hatred, revenge, pettiness of character. And the fruits of forgiveness—humility, compassion, love, peace—are lost to us. The place to begin is not self-condemnation, but the sincere desire to begin anew. If we earnestly seek to forgive, if we seek a change of heart, we will at some point have what we seek, for the nature of God is love, is forgiveness. We ourselves are forgiven even before we think to ask. We don't have to earn it. We just have to be willing to receive. As we ourselves are forgiven, we can through that same fount of grace forgive the injuries done to us.

CHURCHES PREFER CHARITY TO JUSTICE

HUFFINGTON POST

2011

When I was a young adult in New Orleans, I attended a prestigious church which fronted on elegant St. Charles Avenue. One Sunday there was a call from the pulpit for used shoes to be donated to the forgotten souls in the parish prison, one of the worst prisons in Louisiana, and I suppose in the United States. I remember being appalled. After church I went to the minister and asked, "This is a large, powerful church. Why don't we demand that the authorities clothe the prisoners properly?" The minister looked at me and said, "All I know is that some prisoners need some shoes." I never forgot that moment.

Churches almost always prefer charity to justice. Let's take, for example, the question of hunger. Churches find it easier to open a soup kitchen, rather than lobby politicians or put pressure on government to feed hungry people or help them get jobs. I must confess at this point that I, too, give money to charity. But just this morning as I once again wrote a check to the food bank, I note that every year there are more hungry people in my state of Oregon. Last year 240,000 people used the food bank, compared to 200,000 the previous year. What's wrong with this picture? To effect change, churches must move beyond charity to justice, changing the economic and political systems that keep people impoverished.

I don't wish to say that all charitable giving is wrong. Certainly, if we have more than we need, we should give some of the excess away. And there is a sound argument for hands-on work by churches, for the act of serving soup to impoverished people gives middle-class people some sense of what the less fortunate are facing in their everyday lives. These experiences may very well motivate individuals to advocate for policy change. So yes, write the check, serve the soup, but don't stop there.

The problem with charity, including charitable deeds done by churches, is that it allows people to believe that a given social problem is being addressed, when actually there is only a Band-Aid being put on the wound. It allows donors to feel good because they think that they have "made a difference." Actually, charity may do more for the donors than for the institutions they purport to serve. The problems that people face in a country like ours, in which there is such a wide disparity of wealth, cannot be addressed comprehensively by charities, no matter how many people of good will donate or volunteer. Charities act unilaterally and piecemeal, and they tend to serve the sexy causes (i.e., anything to do with children), rather than those less emotionally compelling (e.g., homeless mentally ill men).

When I became a parish minister, I began to understand why almost universally churches will avoid political action in favor of charitable deeds. For one thing, churches are populated mostly by middle-class people, who are relatively comfortable. And ministers of these institutions value stability more than mission. We professional leaders are reluctant to do anything that would cause conflict or controversy in our churches, fearing an institutional split—or at the very least, a reduction of gifts to the church.

Some church people wrongly believe that churches will lose their tax-exempt status if they take a stand on political matters. But the tax code is clear: churches and ministers may speak out at will on any issue, so long as they do not engage in partisan politics—that is, advocate for one candidate over another.

Other people believe that politics is worldly and not therefore suitable for an institution given to spiritual endeavors. Realistically, however, we must understand that politics determines everything from assuring that we have clean drinking water to deciding when we go to war. And politics determines how the abundant resources of this country are shared—or not shared. These issues, which are decided in the political arena, have moral dimensions which churches can hardly ignore, if we are to be taken seriously as a religious people.

Church is not just a place where good friends gather to support one another; it is not a place where people go to save their own souls, and ignore the very real pain of their neighbors; it is not a place to maintain nice, middle-class values. The Holy Spirit is not on the side of stability. Jesus did not say, "I have come that you might be comfortable." He said, "I have come that you may have life." Church is a place to take the demands of justice seriously, and to trouble the waters, when necessary. Will there be controversy? Maybe so. But there will be integrity, there will be mission, there will be life.

FINDING GOD AT THE MARGINS

HUFFINGTON POST

2011

My sister Donna and I recently took a self-guided blues tour of the Mississippi Delta. It was an extraordinary experience. I grew up in the South, but never visited the Delta, the emotional heart of the blues, which runs from Vicksburg, Mississippi, to Memphis, Tennessee. This is rich land that former slaves worked as tenant farmers. The area has a history of slavery, followed by Jim Crow and the Ku Klux Klan. It was and still is characterized by illiteracy, poverty and steaming hot weather. It is also noted for some of the most authentic and moving music made anywhere in our country. Most people will recognize some of the names associated with the area, such as B.B. King and Muddy Waters. If you know about the history of the blues, you will have heard of Charley Patton, Robert Johnson and Son House—early blues musicians, all from the Delta, and now long gone, but still influencing American music.

We started our tour in Ocean Springs, Mississippi, where my sister lives, and worked our way north. We had only five days, so we missed a lot, and never made it to Memphis, but what we saw and heard touched me and changed me. Greenville and the Walnut Street Blues Club was our first stop, where the legendary

John Horton band was playing. The music was loud and the cigarette smoke was heavy. We settled tentatively into a back table, wondering if we could really handle this scene, but the sound soon drew us in. When the band took a break, Horton invited other musicians in the house to make music—a guitarist and then a singer, both nondescript black men with amazing talent, took the stage. I wondered what other musical wonders might be lounging around in the club. We were hooked. Our tour had begun.

From Greenville we went north to Cleveland, Mississippi, and then onto Clarksdale, where we dropped in on Morgan Freeman's Ground Zero Blues Club—unfortunately, on an off night. We went on to Red's, which is a real juke joint, with absolutely no commercial flavor. We had trouble finding the place, which was across some railroad tracks, unlit on the outside and looked as if it were boarded up. Finally we saw the one word RED'S in red paint on the door, so we ventured in. Red himself was behind the bar, and silently waved me off when I offered plastic for a beer. Watermelon Slim was playing, and he is the real deal. He played with his guitar on his lap, and made it hunger and sing with a pick and a miniature whiskey bottle.

What struck me about our trip to the Delta was the amazing music that comes out of this poverty-stricken area. The blues has a distinctive sound, a kind of sweet yearning which comes from the flattened notes, plus the crushing and the sliding. Singers go to the heart of our pain: desire and betrayal and love gone wrong. Acceptance is there, and humor. The music is raw, and it is real. So much in our lives these days is the opposite – fabricated, stripped of true emotional content. This music of the Delta is from the heart, with nothing held back. It reached a place in me where few other art forms are able to go. I think that maybe its power comes from the universality of the feelings expressed. No matter what station in life we hold, all human beings long and all human beings lose. Maybe the hard lives of these people in this hardscrabble place enables them to express with more honesty and power what we all experience.

The other interesting thing is that these clubs and juke joints we visited are the most racially integrated places I have ever been. And we're talking here about Mississippi, a state in a part of the country so widely reviled for its racism. I experienced black and white musicians playing together, and black and white patrons gathered together listening to the music. Perhaps it is the music and its acknowledgment of the common human experience that has drawn the races together here in Mississippi. As a Southerner who grew up with terrible divisions of race, I felt some little piece of healing in this coming together of the races.

I know I have been changed in some subtle way by my trip to the Delta. The music touched some deep place in me that wants to be authentic, that is weary of the deep divisions of race and class in our country, that is tired of the superficiality of most of American culture. Of course, it is because of my class privilege that I had the resources of time and money to travel to Mississippi, to stay in nicely appointed motels, and to seek out the most nurturing food available during my journey. I have returned home now to my safe and warm home in progressive Portland, Oregon, where I can if I wish play my blues CDs in comfort, and remember.

But I can, if I choose to do so, find a way to be in relationship with those on the margins. They are the truth tellers: the hopelessly addicted, the single mom who can't feed her children, the one who is dying without friends or family. I could visit the tent city that is Occupy Portland. There I would find committed young people who are drawing the nation's attention to the crack in our Liberty Bell—and the tents also include mentally ill and homeless folks, who have nowhere else to go. These campers are making their own kind of music: it is dissonant to this radically unequal culture, and we need to hear it.

Why is it that we must go to the margins of society to find what is real? Perhaps it is only at the margins where people have so little to lose that they are free of pretense, unwilling to play the games which draw the rest of us in too much of the time. My trip to the Delta reminded me that when I hold myself away from those who struggle just to get through the day, I am the one who loses the most. If I am looking for redemption, this is where I am most likely to find it.

SAYING GOODBYE TO TOLERANCE

HUFFINGTON POST

2012

I am a Unitarian Universalist, and we consider ourselves the most tolerant of faiths. In the 19th century Universalist churches were known for opening their doors to dissenters of all varieties, and our modern-day UU churches have continued to provide space for those who cannot find a welcome mat elsewhere: atheists and agnostics, religious humanists, political dissidents. We UUs see ourselves as "broadminded," and so tend to say things like, "There is truth in every religious tradition. We respect all religious beliefs." In one of our services, you might hear a reading from the Bible, but just as likely from the Quran, Black Elk, Lao-tse or Starhawk. However, in spite of our long history and tradition of tolerance, I am finding myself increasingly intolerant—specifically, of the theology and practice of many evangelical Christians.

I say this with some real sorrow, and some measure of guilt. I was brought up Southern Baptist, and the church nurtured me and cared for me as I grew up without a mother in a small town in North Louisiana. I owe that church a lot. Some of my relatives remain in fundamentalist-evangelical churches. A professor at a local conservative evangelical seminary has reached out to me in friendship and has asked me several times to speak to his World Religions class. He published my response to one of his essays in a recent book on Christology. He is a good man. He wants his students to know that our world is multi-cultural and to understand and respect the different faiths and ethnic groups they will encounter in the real world, outside the seminary. He and I have had long theological conversations over coffee, and because of his progressive beliefs about environmental issues, I suggested him as a speaker at our UU national conference a few years ago, where he was well received.

The last time my friend asked me to speak, however, I refused. I find myself in the strange position of being a liberal who is closed, in relationship with a theologically conservative evangelical who is open. I'm having to ask myself why.

I thought about my visits with his students over the past few years. To me, a seminary is a place where students open themselves to new ideas, where they question received beliefs. Seminary changes people who attend, sometimes radically. When I visited my friend's class, I did not try to convince students that Unitarian Universalism was the faith they should adopt—I just gave a review of our history and tradition. But as I have tried to explain to my friend, during those visits I always felt like "an insect under glass." The students were unfailingly polite. They smiled. They were not confrontative in the least. The closest comment that came to confrontation was the honest, halting expression of one young woman who closed out the discussion by saying, "I just wish . . . I just wish . . . you believed . . . more like I do." I could see that she was concerned for me, maybe concerned even for my soul, which she no doubt thought would be burning in hell upon my demise. Each time I visited, I went away depressed and discouraged. I wanted curiosity, passionate discussion, even a reasoned rejection. Instead, the students put up a glass shield I couldn't penetrate.

But my classroom experience is not the only reason I have lost tolerance for this brand of Christianity. Conservative evangelical

Christians are sure that they are right about so much, but from my vantage point, much of what they believe is unloving and in fact destructive. I'm thinking about my two nephews. One is a handsome, talented, funny, warm human being who happens to be gay. His older brother is also handsome and talented, but he is a jock sports star and business man—and in his case, a conservative Christian who lives in the Deep South. The older brother will not speak to his younger brother, nor allow his four children to see their uncle, presumably because they might be adversely influenced. The brothers' alienation is deeply hurtful to my sister, the boys' mother. The older brother's attitudes are culturally influenced in a region that is profoundly, fervently conservative, both socially and theologically.

Of even more concern is the preponderance of hate crimes being committed against gays and other minorities. There were 6,628 hate crimes reported in 2010 (the last year data was available), 47 percent race-related; 20 percent religion; 19 percent sexual orientation; 13 percent ethnicity or national origin. According to the Southern Poverty Law Center, 1,018 active hate groups were operating in the United States in 2011, a 60 percent increase since 2000.

Is it fair to blame these crimes on conservative Christianity? Not directly. No doubt, the great majority of people who commit hate crimes would not call themselves Christians of any variety. Indeed, conservative Christians typically say that although they may disagree with the sexual orientation or religion of another, they "hate the sin and love the sinner." In fact, they may go so far as to say that they themselves are "sinners saved by grace." However, I would maintain that these Christians, almost all of whom condemn gays for loving differently, support and perpetuate the milieu in which hate crimes take place. They contribute immensely to the cultural ground out of which prejudice grows and flourishes.

Ministers, respected authority figures in conservative evangelical churches and related institutions all over the country, are preaching their theology of singularity. To be sure, some evangelicals, such as my friend the seminary professor, are encouraging their people to be more like Jesus in terms of social justice and to be more protective of God's green earth. These "new evangelicals" are a growing subset of evangelicals who are changing the religious conversation in conservative circles.

But my friend is a theological conservative, and so far as I know, all conservative evangelicals believe there is but one way to salvation: through faith in Jesus as your personal savior. That stance turns everyone else into an infidel. An unbeliever. A moral pervert. A sinner doomed by God to everlasting punishment. So if these "others" are offending God by their sins and are on their way to hell, what covert permission is being given to those inclined to act violently on their prejudices?

Oppression could be thought of as on a continuum, with one end of that continuum being genocide and the other being more "acceptable" forms, like jokes making fun of minorities, women and gays. Somewhere in the middle is the silence, the refusal to speak out against prejudice, of which Martin Luther King, Jr. said the following: "History will have to record that the greatest tragedy . . . was not the strident clamor of the bad people but the appalling silence of the good people."

All religious traditions are not equal. Some beliefs foster freedom, growth and a deepening of compassion. Others are rigid and exclusive, warning of eternal punishment for those who don't believe in the one true path to salvation, as they see it, or for those who love someone of the same sex. For the personal support the church of my childhood gave me, I remain thankful. I'm sure many conservative evangelicals today feel similar gratitude for their community. But for the damage that conservative Christianity does to people and for its perpetuation of prejudice and hate, I must reject this tradition. I believe those who teach it and preach it are doing great harm, and I in no way wish to be an ally.

THE SEXUALITY OF JESUS

HUFFINGTON POST

2012

Karen L. King, a professor at Harvard Divinity School, has caused quite an uproar with her discovery of a scrap of fourth-century papyrus that suggests Jesus may have been married. She is not the first to speculate about Jesus's marital state—various theologians as well as writers of fiction have suggested that Jesus was married, or gay, or bisexual. King is the first with primary evidence that may be credible, though not definitive, as she has conceded.

The significance of King's discovery is that it has pushed both Christians and non-Christians to think about Jesus as a sexual being. Christian tradition, in avoiding the question and seeing Jesus as asexual or anti-sexual, has been guilty of failing to make him fully human. How did this tradition develop?

Although the earliest Church was Jewish, the Gospel was being preached chiefly to the Gentiles. They were immersed in Greco-Roman philosophical ethics, which posited the dualism of body and soul. Paul himself had studied widely in this tradition and the impact of that philosophy shows up clearly in his teachings. He saw the body as a hindrance to the spirit—at best a temporary housing for the soul.

Control of their followers, including sexual control, was

essential for the early Church, because of their conviction that they were in the "end time." Modern-day readers of the Scripture often greatly underestimate the importance of the eschatological time frame of the early Christians. Sexual abstinence was practiced not because of some imagined abstinence of Jesus, but rather because these Christians thought earthly time was limited. Also, perhaps early Christians wanted to set themselves apart from the known sexual excesses of the Roman world.

Augustine of Hippo (354-430), arguably the most influential theologian of Christendom, answered the question "How are we to be saved?" from a Platonic perspective. He propagated the belief that the sex act itself was sinful, and that original sin was transmitted by concupiscence. So, for Augustine, we poor humans are inherently sinful. Since Jesus was perfect and without sin, it follows that he must have been conceived by God and born of a virgin—and needless to say, never had sexual feelings himself.

So Augustine's unfortunate premise and shaky logic calls into question human sexuality, per se: it follows that those who strive for the purity of Jesus would look upon their sexual impulses as sinful. We use sex for pleasure as well as procreation, of course, but often the pleasure is laced with guilt, and we find ourselves unable to celebrate sex with our whole being. Instead of integrating our sexuality with our spirituality, the cultural norm evidences a striking incompatibility of our sexual impulses with our yearning for God. Women are reduced to the virgin and the whore. In spite of the supposed freedom of young women to indulge in loose sexuality liaisons, the double standard still reigns: bad girls are for sex, good girls are for marriage. How many synonyms for "slut" do you know?

Was Jesus married? The Gospels are silent about the subject. But as William Phipps argued long ago ("Was Jesus Married," Harper & Row, 1970), Jesus most likely followed the expected pattern of conduct for a young man in ancient Judaism, which was to be betrothed shortly after puberty. In fact, marriage was not a question to be determined by a Hebrew boy; rather it was his father's duty to betroth his son. The average age of marriage for boy was 16 and the age of betrothal even younger. We know that Jesus was circumcised at the age prescribed and that he was taught Scripture and apprenticed as a carpenter. Is it not reasonable, then, to believe he was an obedient son in being betrothed and later married? Of course it is difficult for some Christians to accept the fact that Jesus was throughout his life a Jew.

Certainly Jesus's open, easy, egalitarian relationships with women were unconventional. He was known to consort openly with prostitutes. He drew many faithful women followers, who were apparently treated as equal to his male disciples. This accepting attitude of Jesus toward women stands in great contrast to the heavily patriarchal Hebrew practice of his day.

Even a cursory view of the Scripture shows us Jesus to be intensely alive, vital and responsive. He had a strong sense of humor, and he was certainly no ascetic: Jesus in fact was criticized by his enemies for being a "glutton and a wine-bibber." He enjoyed the company, conversation and the celebration of marriage feasts. He was forever eating and drinking in many various homes, of Saints and sinners alike, during his ministry. He was pleased and delighted to be anointed with sweet smelling oil.

Moreover, Jesus was keenly aware of the natural world: the reaping of grain, the sheep in the fold, the sparrows' flight in the marketplace, the wind listing where it will. The images in many of his parables are drawn from the sensual pleasures of everyday life. Surely we can conclude from the evidence that Jesus was very much in touch with the erotic dimension—that is, the life force within him. To believe that he could be this responsive to his immediate environment and be unaware of himself as a sexual being is highly unlikely. Chances are that this very sensual man was moved to sexual desire easily and frequently.

Typically, Christians are afraid of Jesus's humanity, preferring to see him as a Divine stick figure without the usual human flesh and frailty. Why does this image persist? Perhaps it is because we know all too well the failures and inconsistencies of the flesh. We know we are animals, we know the ways in which our physical needs and desires upset our equilibrium. Could Jesus really have awakened with an erection, or desired a sensuous woman in the marketplace? Blasphemy! To conceive of Jesus struggling in the same way we do is unthinkable.

Maybe these images seem blasphemous to us because we don't want a God clothed in flesh. We cannot accept incarnation—we need a God "up there," perfect in beauty and form. We deny Jesus's humanity because we cannot stand his likeness to us. In Jesus, God is saying to us, "Accept your own sacredness and beauty! This is what it can mean to be human!" But we turn away, afraid.

The Jesus I know is robust—a carpenter, capable of doing heavy work. He is a fleshly man, filled with thankfulness for the beauty of the natural world, and one who enjoys good food and drink. He is a man of great tenderness, not ashamed of his tears. He does not hide his feelings, and goes straight to the heart in a few words. The Jesus I know enjoys his body and is aware of the wonders of its shape and movement, likes to feel the sun on his limbs, takes pleasure in resting after a long day's journey. He likes the feel of splashing water on his skin when he washes.

And he is a sexual man, one who enjoys being a man, including having a penis, though it is sometimes troublesome for him, demanding attention when he wants to be otherwise occupied. But he accepts that as simply part of what is, like being thirsty or feeling weary or getting angry. Sexuality is part of being human, and it's good.

In his remarkable self-acceptance, Jesus seems to bring new life to whoever comes near. His presence is extraordinarily vital, is fearsome, and calls for a profound response. Jesus is in fact God's invitation to wholeness and self-hood. When we are able to celebrate Jesus in the flesh, we understand that we, too, are called to incarnation, called to embody God's Spirit in our earthly form. Perhaps this challenge is too daunting, so we prefer to strip Jesus of his humanness and to deny our own potential for divinity. Karen King has asked us to consider what we have lost.

THE EMERGENCE OF THE FEMININE

HUFFINGTON POST

2013

What is going on? Two male icons of religion have made surprising, and gratifying, pronouncements of late. Pope Francis says he is not going to judge gay priests and furthermore stated that the church needs a "theology of women." The Dalai Lama just made an even more shocking statement. When asked if the next Dalai Lama could be female, he said, "If a female Dalai Lama is needed, one will appear."

But should we be so surprised? Maybe these statements were inevitable. Maybe we are seeing some stirring in the collective psyche, some divine movement in the unconscious signaling the waning strength of the masculine principle. Patriarchy has definitely worn out its virtues.

Intuitively, we know that we are out of right relationship, with one another and with the earth. In quiet moments, we know our pain. Our dreams are troubled. When our ways no longer serve life, the new appears.

The emerging shift is towards balance—a balance of the masculine and feminine modes of consciousness, of anima and animus, of yin and yang, both in the culture at large and within our personal lives as well. The signs are everywhere. The distrust of absolute authority, whether it be with our physicians or our ministers and priests. The passionate interest in protecting the earth. The rising consciousness about race and class and an understanding that exclusivity impoverishes us all. The insistence that people with disabilities have access to learning and to pleasure. The embracing of people of various sexual orientations. Gender roles freeing us to live in accordance with our talents and desires.

My perspective is Jungian, which assumes archetypes, or universal patterns in the human psyche. These patterns are not, of course, restricted to sex or gender, and both are present in both women and men. In psychospiritual language, the terms *masculine* and *feminine* delineate the opposite energies which give necessary tension and therefore vitality to our lives—the electrical poles of the psyche that charge us and energize us.

If an individual remains unconscious of one of these realms of energy, then they project all the gifts of that pole onto another. When such projection occurs on the cultural level, women carry the qualities of the anima, such as intuiting, caring, and feeling, whereas men carry the animus qualities of initiating, task-orientation, and analytical thinking. When individuals become conscious, however, of both these poles of psychic energy, then each person develops more fully, in wherever ways they feel moved, not having to suppress inclinations and talents because of rigid gender roles and expectations.

As children grow and develop, the traditional cultural pattern is for both sexes to acknowledge certainly by adolescence that the male is the norm, and that the female's proper place is to carry the male's shadow side—that is, the feeling, nurturing side. The female is now discovering her warrior side, her dark energy, and using assertive, linear male energy for her own ends. The male, then, is no longer able to project the anima outward and so is having to discover and integrate the feminine into his personality. We see women working on construction sites now, and men pushing past with strollers.

I should clarify that I am not talking about feminism, per se. Many variants of feminism have emerged, some of them having less to do than others with this psychic shift. I am not speaking of a coup in which one gender overturns the power of the other and takes over. I am not speaking of the rule of the goddess, nor of breaking the glass ceiling of the Fortune 500 companies. I'm not speaking even of "leaning in."

I am speaking of a spiritual revolution that radically changes how we see ourselves in relation to others, a revolution that begins with the kind of internal change that Jesus was talking about when he said, "Ye must be born again." Born into a new way of seeing. Understanding that there is no stranger, no "other." It will not be enough to say away with injustice, down with economic inequity—spread out the goodies in a more equitable manner. This revolution is about seeing another as one's self. It's about leaving behind a way of relating in which we judge and classify but neglect to experience and love.

The masculine principle is characterized by analytic thinking, independence, linearity, innovation, assertion, abstract ethical thought, concern with law and order. It initiates, it thrusts, it enters, it stands, it commands. It is the skyscraper, the rocket, the racing car, the smoking gun. This principle concerns itself with clarity and moderation, is wary of an excess of emotion which might cloud one's thinking. It is part of a tradition that we could call heroic and calls for will, honor, strength, and sacrifice to an ideal. It is the individual seeker going after the Holy Grail, fighting off the dragons, and saving the town. It is the gunfighter that risks his life at O.K. Corral. It is the Odysseus returning home from war.

Whereas the feminine principle draws us to all living things, respecting nature and honoring nature's mysteries, the masculine principle penetrates and dissects those mysteries. The feminine takes in and includes, the masculine excludes by dividing and categorizing. The feminine principle speaks to the soul's need for emotion, spontaneity, ecstasy. Subjective feelings and intuition are seen as paths to knowing. The body/mind split, so pervasive in our culture for so long, is rejected. The anima affirms what is not I, affirms an underlying unity to all of life. It is mutual and it is participatory. It is relational in all matters, and relationship is not a means to an end, but exists for its own sake. We are called to be present in the moment, in the sensual, in our messy and imperfect flesh, rather than experiencing life from the aesthetic perfection of abstract law and principle.

Note that I am not claiming that the masculine principle is inferior, and the feminine principle, superior. In fact, if we are looking at this shift as a necessary evolution in time, we see that the dominance of the masculine had its place, had its day. Refusing to allow emotion to dominate thinking, organizing groups to an end, adhering to codes of honor—these principles have brought advances that were crucial to our survival at one point. But times have changed, and an overweening masculine principle is no longer adaptive.

The excess of the masculine principle in American culture is all too apparent: in our de-sacralizing of the earth, turning her gifts of life into products for short-term gain; in filling our air and food and water with noxious chemicals, then spending billions of dollars trying to cure cancer; in conducting a foreign policy which is devoid of relational principle, and focused on the clear and unambiguous ends of gain for American business, in spite of the human toll. The necessity of the feminine is now both obvious and urgent.

This cultural shift offers to us—both men and women—a chance to recover the riches we have disowned and bring their power and beauty into our consciousness. We are being given an invitation to wholeness, to right relationship. The sacred feminine, the Dark Yin, can show us how to heal and how to redeem the world.

Of course cultural change is always accompanied by fear and trepidation. We have seen a ferocious backlash, with Fundamentalist Christian groups withdrawing into their safe assurances and dogma, withdrawing their children from the evil influences of public schools, and insisting that their women learn once again the godly lessons of submission. Fashion advertising portrays women as fragile, child-like, whereas popular movies ironically feature female anti-heroes with as much destructive capability as male heroes. The Republican Party has become the party of old white men as it tries to maintain its hold on the past. But history is quickly leaving them behind as women, people of color, gays, transgender people, and the young insist on a future more just and more diverse. Old assumptions die hard, and we strain to hear one another. This is not an easy time for those of us caught in these shifting sands, but nonetheless exhilarating.

The shift is coming, but will it come soon enough? Regressive social and economic forces are strong—there is the very real possibility is that multinational corporations will become a Hydra that cannot be stopped, gobbling up resources and despoiling the earth, accountable to no one and directed only by its own appetite. Horrified, we watch the glaciers melt, the forests burn, species disappear. Writers as diverse as Barbara Kingsolver, Cormac McCarthy, Naomi Shihab Nye, and Sherman Alexie are warning us: the house is on fire!

As we move into this new way of being, balancing the male and the female principles, where does theology come in? What about the church? This is not the time for safety, for pleasing the people in the pews. This is the time for prophecy. We must set our imaginations loose and dream a world that is possible. We must create language that is not the language of domination, as Riane Eisler suggests in her work on cultural transformation. We must look to our poets and our mystics to discover different metaphors that structure and determine our thoughts and behavior.

The recent statements of Pope Francis and the Dalai Lama are unprecedented and provocative. The question for religious people of every stripe and persuasion is whether we will be a regressive force, supporting the status quo, or whether we will understand that a life-giving revolution is at hand and become participant in that change. We need the increased influence of the feminine principle, sooner rather than later. In fact, later may be too late.

CLIMATE CHANGE: THEOLOGICAL CONSIDERATIONS

HUFFINGTON POST

2016

My husband and I went on a long-planned trip to lovely Charleston, South Carolina, last October—as it turned out, just as the city's most recent flood was subsiding. The local paper (*The Post and Courier*) reported one of highest tides on record, swamping cars, creeping into homes, and tangling traffic. Hundreds of people who live near the edge of the water in this tourist area couldn't get to work. I chatted with the wait staff in restaurants, as I sought out the shrimp po boys, the collard greens, the fried chicken I love: *Are you concerned about global warming?* Typically, the answer was "No, flooding is a regular occurrence, we are used to it."

Day after day comes the influx of bad news about climate. Since the Paris agreement of last December (COP21), climate scientists have told us (1) 2015 was the warmest year ever, by far, (2) tidal flooding is increasing problematic in coastline cities, (3) if current carbon emissions continue, the West Antarctic ice sheet could begin to fragment, causing a rise of five to six feet in sea level by the end of this century, and (4) these shifts could be abrupt, giving us little time to prepare. Scientists are not talking about two hundred years from now—all this could happen within the lifetime of children born today. As I write, my fear ratchets up, my breath grows light. I recall the words of poet friend when I asked her if she thought we could avoid climate catastrophe: "Humans are a very flawed species."

Even the most balanced writers cannot be optimistic. William Nordhaus (*The Climate Casino: Risk, Uncertainty, and Economics for a Warming World*), one of the world's leading economic thinkers on climate change, believes it is possible to keep the worst from happening, with relatively small economic cost—but fears that the political will is not there. Environmental ethicist Dale Jamieson (*Reason in a Dark Time: Why the Struggle Against Climate Change Failed—and What It Means for Our Future*) writes, "Sadly, it is not entirely clear that democracy is up to the challenge of climate change," pointing out that powerful economic and political interests benefit from the activities that cause climate change, while the costs are borne by others.

Holding the rise in the earth's temperature to 2 degrees Celsius will not prevent the damage already done, damage that will continue to affect our earth for thousands of years. We have already seen the punishing heat waves, the melting of the glaciers, the fierce storms, the rising flood waters. If we exceed the Paris target and coastlines go under water, we will see food and water shortages that will make the current emigrant crisis seem simple to address. We will see the increase of tribalism and armed conflict as suffering and frightened people vie for control of resources. Why have so many books and films of late portrayed the apocalypse? Because art is prophetic of what is to come.

I am a minister, and hopeful by nature. However, I am also a realist, and I'm guessing that we're in for a pile of trouble. Emissions in China and India and other developing countries are rising. Population growth is expected to peak at about 9.5 billion by 2050, from the present 7 billion, straining the planet's resources further. The World Economic Forum recently put climate change at the top of its risk list. Cecilia Reyes, who helped develop the report, said, "Climate change is exacerbating more risks than ever before in terms of water crises, food shortages, constrained economic growth, weaker social cohesion and increased security risks."

Given the nature of the beast, then, how are people of faith called to respond? What are the theological implications?

This would not be the first time that theological revisioning has been called for—throughout history, seismic shifts in political and economic realms have called into question theological beliefs which previously brought people some modicum of comfort and certainty. Consider the Enlightenment, which took God out of the center and placed the human there; the American and French revolutions and the rise of democracy; World War II, with the creation of the atomic bomb and the unthinkable evil of the holocaust. The technological transformations of our own post-industrial age push forward relentlessly, asking not *why*, but only *how* and *when*: machines take the place of workers; globalization rewards and punishes, creating vast economic disparity; new media bring the suffering of others around the world into our homes; knowledge is exploding, while wisdom lags way behind.

At such times of transition, our faith is shaken, even shattered. We drift aimlessly, wondering how to bring our given beliefs in line with the reality of our existential experience. Of all the changes we currently face, that of a warming planet is the most unnerving: *the 21st century is the first time in the history of the world that one generation has been given the task of keeping our planet viable, not just for ourselves, but for generations to come.* We are being called upon, once again, to reimagine our theology, to question what we hold sacred, for these beliefs determine our working definition of morality and dictate how we actually behave.

I suggest the following considerations. Our theology must become:

Radically relational. Because global warming is a phenomenon shared by all peoples in all places, we no longer can think of ourselves as independent agents, or in fact "exceptional," either as individuals or as countries. What touches one, touches all. In a country in which individual striving is paramount, we need to reconsider the whole concept of salvation. What does it mean to be "saved"? We can no longer conceive of ourselves as being saved alone—our connectedness is radical and undeniable. The coal we burn today turns into somebody's else's storm thousands of miles away. We continue to drive gasoline-powered cars, and island countries disappear. The coastline of Florida may very well go underwater in fifty years—or much sooner. A hundred years from now? Our world becomes unthinkable.

Respectful of the natural world. Christians have too long interpreted the book of Genesis as giving humans dominion over all of nature, to use as we please. Nature, we are beginning to understand, includes ourselves. We are part of a profoundly interdependent creation, and we interact intrinsically with all other forms of life, in both space and time. When we relate to the earth as utilitarian, as a means to an end, the earth becomes "other" and subject to all kinds of abuse. We would do well to learn what indigenous people have been trying to tell us since we began to exploit the earth they hold sacred. Greed is not good, contrary to what the fictional Gordon Gekko and his counterparts on Wall Street believe. Conquering and taking must give way to a theology of humility and repentance.

Informed by the sensory world and the arts, not just the world of weights and measurements. Scientific positivism has brought its gifts, its amazing productivity, but this is merely one dimension to consider, one measure of the good life. On the other hand, poets, visual artists, filmmakers wake us up to the magnificence of our earth and its sacredness. When our interactions with nature are sensory—when our hand touches the bark of an old-growth tree, when we step with bare feet into a stream, when we see a sunrise streaking the sky with red and pink and orange—we understand nature as a primal force which brings both great joy and great responsibility.

Inclusive of civic life, a perspective that encourages and empowers us as citizens, not just of our city or state or country, but citizens of the world. More than ever before, we are called to take responsibility for the "commons," a term which is derived from the Latin *communis*, originally meaning "sharing common duties." In an era in which vast amounts of public wealth have been transferred into private hands, a time in which money rules politics so completely, we must hold sacred the right of all people to participate in the life of the state. Our morality must not be constrained by skin color, religious persuasion, language, gender, ethnic or class background. It's not enough to say "my children," "my neighborhood," "my town," rather recognizing that when any child lacks food or a safe place to live or a decent education, then the body politic suffers, and we all are diminished. Our connectedness to all living things will become more and more apparent, as will our dependency upon one another. A civic theology will ask us to enlarge our sense of the commons, to make our caring universal rather than exclusive.

Conscious of generational justice, considering not just the suffering of those alive now, but the needs of many generations to come. Evolution has produced human beings who are hard-wired to fear the moment, to act in our own immediate self-interest, as a survival instinct. We can hardly conceive of next week, much less 50 or 100 or 200 years from now. But there is no doubt that the decisions we make today will determine the kind of existence possible for many, many generations to come.

I remember being moved by Robert Flaherty's *Nanook of the North*, a film that is often referred to as the first documentary. The protagonist, Nanook, moves through the wilderness of Northern Canada, hunting, fishing, building an igloo. This Inuit considers the next hunter or fisherman who may happen by, and leaves each shelter or site more hospitable than when he found it. He sees himself as responsible for those unknown ones who will come. Our ethic of stewardship must extend to those nameless ones who will follow, those who will be born and live and love and die largely dependent upon our care for the earth they happen into. For those we don't know and will never know, we must be ever vigilant, fiercely protective.

Foolishly, irrationally hopeful, because we do not have the luxury of despair. What is the source of this imprudent hope? It is grounded in the life force itself, and in the faith that is called forth when we face impossible odds, odds that would make any halfway reasonable person admit defeat. It is the hope of the children of Israel wandering lost, forsaken, in a barren land. It is the hope of the shepherd boy David as he chooses a stone for his sling and trembling, looks up at Goliath. It is the preposterous hope of Jesus, as he prays in the garden of Gethsemane. We are called simply to be faithful. We cannot count on the fruits of our labor. We do what is right solely because it is right. Our faith stands in contrast to all that which takes, devours, destroys. It is sustained by love, for the earth and all living things. It is larger than self.

Someone has said that this is a good time in history to be alive. I think I understand that sentiment. The climate crisis has given our generation a great deal of clarity about moral purpose. We have challenges that can bring out the best in us, engendering a great storm of creativity and compassion. We are facing a behemoth of destruction, almost beyond imagination, that demands a kind of faithfulness like no other we have known. We are called forth, to be bigger than we are. Yes, it is a good time to be alive.

Our situation reminds me of when I was a young woman, and so joyfully pregnant. I had no question about the meaning of my life. I gave myself away to purposes larger than my own pleasure, my own safety, even. I knew I was a container of life. I still am. So are all of us.

www.ingramcontent.com/pod-product-compliance
Lightning Source LLC
Chambersburg PA
CBHW021702110726
47902CB00007B/2025
* 9 7 8 0 9 9 6 1 0 4 0 7 4 *